OCD TREATMENT

A Helpful Book About Obsessive-compulsive Disorder

(A Crash Course to Taking Your Life Back From Obsessive-compulsive Disorder)

Carolyn Arriola

Published By Jordan Levy

Carolyn Arriola

All Rights Reserved

Ocd Treatment: A Helpful Book About Obsessive-compulsive Disorder (A Crash Course to Taking Your Life Back From Obsessive-compulsive Disorder)

ISBN 978-1-77485-273-6

All rights reserved. No part of this guide may be reproduced in any form without permission in writing from the publisher except in the case of brief quotations embodied in critical articles or reviews.

Legal & Disclaimer

The information contained in this book is not designed to replace or take the place of any form of medicine or professional medical advice. The information in this book has been provided for educational and entertainment purposes only.

The information contained in this book has been compiled from sources deemed reliable, and it is accurate to the best of the Author's knowledge; however, the Author cannot guarantee its accuracy and validity and cannot be held liable for any errors or omissions. Changes are periodically made to this book. You must consult your doctor or get professional medical advice before using any of the suggested remedies, techniques, or information in this book.

Upon using the information contained in this book, you agree to hold harmless the Author from and against any damages, costs, and expenses, including any legal fees potentially resulting from the application of any of the information provided by this guide. This disclaimer applies to any damages or injury caused by the use and application, whether directly or indirectly, of any advice or information presented, whether for breach of contract, tort, negligence, personal injury, criminal intent, or under any other cause of action.

You agree to accept all risks of using the information presented inside this book. You need to consult a professional medical practitioner in order to ensure you are both able and healthy enough to participate in this program.

TABLE OF CONTENTS

INTRODUCTION 1

CHAPTER 1: WHAT'S OCD? 3

CHAPTER 2: THE SECRET MOTIVES FOR OCD... 9

CHAPTER 3: LEARNING TO UNDERSTAND OCD: WHAT IT IS, AND WHAT ISN'T 17

CHAPTER 4: HOW IS OBSESSIVE-COMPULSIVE DISORDER BE DIAGNOSED? 25

CHAPTER 5: THE OCD ISN'T AN IMPAIRMENT. IT'S AN ADVANTAGE 38

CHAPTER 6: THE COMMON OBSESSIONS OF OCD 50

CHAPTER 7: MINDFUL REVIEW 66

CHAPTER 8: TREATMENT OF SYMPTOMS WITH A HEALTHY LIFESTYLE 72

CHAPTER 9: HOW TO GET OCD DIAGNOSED. WAY DOES OCD GET DIAGNOSED AND THEN CONFIRMED 79

CHAPTER 10: CAUSES OF OCD 86

CHAPTER 11: BELIEVE SYSTEM 92

CHAPTER 12: CONTROLLING THE OCD OF YOURSELF 103

CHAPTER 13: THE TREATMENT FOR OCD 109

CHAPTER 14: PREVENTION OF OCD 121

CHAPTER 15: HOW TO DO TO MANAGE OBSESSIVE COMPULSIVE DISORDER? 126

CHAPTER 16: INITIAL TREATMENT: STRATEGIES TO REDUCE THE SYMPTOMS AND EFFECTS OCD YOURSELF.............. 135

CHAPTER 17: THE TOPIC IS COGNITIVE-BEHAVIORAL THERAPY. 150

CHAPTER 18: LIFESTYLE AND HOME REMEDIES FOR OCD 161

CHAPTER 19: RESOLVING THE CONDITION 176

CONCLUSION... 180

Introduction

Obsessive Compulsive Personality Disorder (OCD) is a disorder that can alter your normal well-balanced relationships with family and with your friends. It can also create stress and negatively affect your health, mood and other aspects of your everyday life. It's time to find ways to conquer and manage OCD. It's a challenge, but is it possible to control yourself and conquer OCD?

This book can help you with this. With the right knowledge and the appropriate strategy and determination to adhere to the guidelines in this book, it is easier to attain the success you desire in managing and treating OCD efficiently.

The book will explain everything you need to know about fighting OCD and the things you must take to assist you in reaching your goals. Everything in the text is written using a straightforward written language that anyone is competent to understand even not familiar with medical terms.

Chapter 1: What's Ocd?

Obsessive-compulsive disorder is described as an anxiety-related condition. It may trigger disturbing thoughts and causes you to repeat your actions. One of the most significant features of OCD is that you realize that your thoughts and actions aren't rational but they aren't able to stop them from impacting your everyday life.

Obsessions

It's normal to become overwhelmed by the task of cleaning of your home when there are guests over for dinner. There is also a tendency to have quick, disturbing thoughts about anger, far-fetched fantasies along with other things that we would not normally do. We are perfectionists, and are so focused on the finer details that we try to align every single photo frame on display. We make fun of ourselves and say that"we're "OCD" to do this, but for someone who really suffer from obsessive-compulsive disorder life is difficult and uncomfortable.

These obsessions can be extremely destructive. They appear quickly and overwhelm any attempt to confront them or fight them. If they are mild cases, you may be extremely nervous. The most severe fears could be frightening images of the Devil and violent sexual abuse (even in the event that the individual who is suffering does not take any action upon the thought) A close family member or friend who has passed away suddenly or the notion that inanimate objects are alive.

The most alarming aspect of these thoughts could be the fact that the person who is affected realizes that they aren't real, yet they're incapable of stopping them. It's difficult to stop these disturbing thoughts once they've begun.

Compulsions

Obsessive-compulsive disorders are not always obsessed, however, more than half of people affected by OCD are compelled to perform routine chores and rituals. Compulsive behaviors may take many forms. The most well-known topics include counting, cleaning or examining, seeking assurance, putting things in the right place in a silent manner, repeating words and hoarding. being too focused or creating neutralizing thoughts to prevent engaging in obsessive thoughts and also avoid situations that cause obsessive thoughts.

Television and in movies of individuals who suffer from OCD often show the sufferer performing the act of compulsion but rarely show the extreme anxiety that comes with the disorder. In the real world,

OCD sufferers repeat compulsive actions in an attempt to ease some of the anxiety. They are made to behave in a way that is against their will, and cannot get relief from their behavior. It is likely that their stress levels may drop one or two minutes.

It's a scary life.

The most common diagnosis for obsessive-compulsive disorder is that obsessions and compulsions are usually one hour per day. In some cases, the obsessions can be severe enough to result in physical injury.

Complications

OCD that is serious can create medical issues. Hand washing repeatedly, for example could leave the skin rough and abrasive. Skin picks may cause cuts and infections that pull hair that can lead to problems as well as hair loss.

Many people suffering from OCD who are not treated OCD are also susceptible to other mental conditions that go beyond skin picking. The most prevalent one is known as major depression. How many people wouldn't feel depressed when faced with these situations? A study that was conducted in 2009 revealed that 50% of OCD sufferers have had suicidal thoughts, and that 15% have attempted suicide. Other mental disorders that could be linked to OCD include eating disorders, sleep disorders, general anxiety, as well as social anxiety disorders. Additionally, they can be affected by addictive behaviors.

The good news is that the majority of people treated for obsessive-compulsive disorder enjoy a higher levels of living. But, they need to remain in contact with medical and mental health professionals, however. OCD is a chronic disease with ups as well as downs.

After we've identified exactly what OCD is, let's examine the reasons behind it.

For healing

Chapter 2: The Secret Motives For Ocd...

Anxiety can arise from every aspect of your life. The only thing to take into consideration is that you're actually confronted by the stressor that you're experiencing and you think you're in a position to manage. The causes of stress are typically classified into four groups including genetics and conditioning and conditions, brain chemistry or personal. Let's take a look at each of these.

Genetics and Conditioning

There are many who believe that there's an important genetic factor that causes the occurrences of OCD But these claims are at present, unproven. There's a high likelihood that you'll be most likely to get OCD in the event that a close member of yours has OCD or has had it. But the reason for this isn't fully understood. It could be due luck, or, more likely, the result of the influence of the people who surround you. Let me review the issue in more detail.

Let's suppose that it was your mom to worry. The anxiety she felt was expressed in many different methods, including doing her best to stay secure and following various daily routines including checking the water supply. The belief was that these routines helped to keep her anxiety under control and also kept her family members were safe. You'd have observed and subconsciously observed the actions she was taking. You noticed (rightly or wrongly) that when you're feeling anxious it's beneficial to do certain things. This means that as you age and mature you're more likely to behave similarly when having similar feelings. You've seen it before and you think this is how you should proceed.

If you feel this seems unrealistic be aware that the vast majority of how your interactions with people around you stems of this type of conditioning. What can the coping strategies for stress and anxiety be different?

Brain Chemistry

Another possible reason one of the reasons for OCD may be due to the existence of a defective brain chemical. In reality the spotlight has been paid to part of the brain in biology as well as the chemistry of recent times. This has allowed us to greatly increase our understanding of OCD and the mental state and how brain processes operate in our brains at any time.

In the beginning the researchers have noticed that the brain cortex of OCD sufferers, that the brain functions in a manner that is somewhat different from the normal human. It is evident by an increase in activities and flow of blood to specific brain regions, as also a decrease in the levels of a neurotransmitter crucially known as serotonin.

Serotonin has a role to play in the regulation of various body functions, including depression, mood memories, anxious and sleep. It's also the main source of depression and various mood-related disorders. A lack of quantities of this substance within the brain may cause issues in the communication between the the frontal cortex and the more complex structures which could lead to problems like yours.

The results of these research studies have led to the most efficient treatments to be selected for those who suffer from an increase in severity of the disorder, including serotonin inhibition of reuptake or Cognitive Behavioral Therapy (CBT). These treatments can all improve blood flow, regulate brain's activity, and increase levels of serotonin inside the brain. We'll discuss ways to do this in the upcoming chapters.

It's unlikely that a chemical imbalance in the brain is the primary reason for obsessive compulsive disorder. But, it certainly influences the severity of the. The condition.

Life Events

Life can get challenging and difficult times can occur. If they do it, they typically test our resilience to the limit. Sometimes, we're not hurt but in other instances such situations place a lot of strain on our body which exhausts its resources which can lead to stress-related anxiety and stress symptoms like yours.

They could be caused by some of the following: neglect, bullies or abuse or even times of stress like having a baby, the move home or getting fired from your position, or the date of your test and so on. There's no single cause and what you perceive as stressful and stressful may differ from other people's experiences.

This doesn't mean you're not as capable as others in your vicinity in the event of stress or anxiety that causes an increase in OCD or anxiety. It also doesn't suggest that it was result of the incident or situation. It's just that it is a crucial factor.

Personality

Your personality could influence how you feel. This is, for instance, if you are inclined to be a perfectionist (someone who is obsessed with accuracy and order) If you are more likely to suffer from stress and anxious, or you like to be in the top position of your game at all times studies have shown that you are more vulnerable to being in pain. This is particularly true when you're struggling with your appearance, as in your self-esteem and mood.

But, it doesn't mean that you are the root cause of the disorder. It's more that you are more susceptible to getting afflicted.

Once you've reached the conclusion of this section you'll be able to gain a better comprehension of the reasons behind your own OCD. Perhaps you have a family member who suffers from anxiety, or perhaps you're prone to perfectionist tendencies , or perhaps you've been the victim of an traumatic incident or suffered endless stress. Maybe your brain's chemical balance is off-balance and you require help to get back on track?

It's probable that one or more of those problems that led you to your job you are currently in. Take some time to think about what the root causes of these problems could be. This short exercise can help you in getting to the root of your issue and assist you in overcoming them.

Now, we'll shift our attention to the most important part in the text: the diagnostic test. Is your condition an obsessive compulsive disorder, or is it something else? Make sure you answer the questions in the next chapter. You will be able to find out!

Chapter 3: Learning to understand Ocd: What It Is, and What Isn't

Out of all health concerns that affect people who suffer from obsessive compulsive disorder (OCD) is likely to be the most well-known of the list. In the recent years, terms such as "obsessive-compulsive" and "OC" have become part of common-use language, routinely used not only by mental health professionals, but by laypeople in everyday conversation as well.

However, the wide usage of terms related to OCD isn't a sign that it's a greater increase in the public's awareness of the nature of OCD. Pop psych articles and other media portrayals have popularized the term "obsessive-compulsive" to describe people who are excessively neat and organized, but are these qualities enough to rightly merit the diagnosis of obsessive-compulsive disorder? What is required to be diagnosed as having OCD and are the signs that you're experiencing enough to warrant an OCD diagnosis? This chapter will help you identify this.

OCD: What Does It Mean?

Obsessive-compulsive disorder (OCD) are defined as a disorder defined by compulsive, obsessive behaviors , or both.

Obsessions are a constant stream of thoughts, images, or feelings. The information they convey varies from person to however the most frequent subjects are those of contamination (e.g. the constant fear of being infected with dirt and bacteria) as well as Symmetry (obsessive thoughts that have a certain pattern and order) and also harm (e.g. thoughts of violence, or fear of hurting yourself or others) and taboo-related aspects (e.g. sexual thoughts or acts of aggression which aren't allowed). These thoughts can be invasive and uncontrollable frequently leading to extreme anxiety and anxiety. To ease the anxiety and stress the sufferers are suffering from these issues attempt to keep them from happening or to eliminate the thoughts by engaging in different activities or thoughts, such as executing routines.

While obsessions are thoughts that repeat and actions, compulsions tend to be more frequent. They are routines that are generally carried out to lessen the anxiety due to obsessions. For instance, excessive hand washing rituals that are used to counter the fear of contamination, or just repeating the same words an equal amount of times to create a symmetry that is obsessive. A person suffering from OCD may also be compelled to comply with compulsions in order to avoid an occurrence that could be terrifying, such as making sure the stove is turned off for twenty times to ward off fears of the house burning down if a medical check-up isn't completed.

The majority of those who suffer from OCD are affected by both compulsions and obsessions It is possible that OCD may be the result of obsessions only or Compulsions. One of the most important criteria to determine if these compulsions are the root cause for OCD is to look at how they impact everyday life. OCD is identified when routines or compulsions continue longer than an hour per day, cause intense distress for the person and/or affect key areas of the life of the individual. This can affect relationships at home or hindering work productivity.

OCD What does it mean? It's Not

To effectively manage OCD to control it, it's essential not to just be aware of what causes it, but also to distinguish OCD from other disorders similar to it and be aware of common beliefs regarding it.

One of the disorders which are frequently mistaken for OCD is OCPD that is also referred to by the name of obsessive-compulsive disorders. If you're not familiar with the mental health field, they might not be aware of the distinct distinction between the two. People often use the terms interchangeably , however, in the real diagnosis, there's a distinction to be drawn. The diagnosis forms the foundation for the treatment plan which is then suggested and then implemented therefore it's crucial to establish if you're experiencing problems with OCD and OCPD.

What's the simplest method of separating these two? One of the most important things to be aware of is that in contrast to

OCD, OCPD does not suffer from obsessions or compulsions. While it's a disorder that is in itself one of control and order and is often characterized by overly perfectionists. OCPD doesn't have frequent intrusive thoughts or desires and it doesn't need regular rituals and actions that are usually used to block out unwanted thoughts.

Furthermore, OCD is differentiated from specific behaviors that are typically defined as "obsessive" (e.g. obsessed with the appearance of a person or collecting things or being obsessed with how one looks) as well as those which have been described by the term "compulsive" (e.g. playing with your friends, lying to yourself or even shopping). These are usually signs of mental health problems that require proper treatment according to the diagnoses and treatments.

OCD, its Involvement, Prevalence and Course

In in the United States, obsessive-compulsive disorder (OCD) is a disorder which is affecting 1.2 percentage of population which is about 12 people per 1,000 people. The proportion of OCD all over the world is estimated to be 1.1 1. 1.8 percent.

The initial symptom of OCD symptoms can be slow, with an average of onset ranging from 19.5 years old. A quarter of OCD cases are diagnosed at the age of 14. The appearance of symptoms after 35 is very uncommon however, it can happen.

If not treated, OCD typically takes on the form of chronic illness which is characterised by symptoms becoming more severe and less over the duration of. Early detection, precise determination of its severity the prompt intervention, and the appropriate treatment are crucial to the treatment rehabilitation and recovery from OCD.

If you've been identified as being suffering from OCD or suspect that OCD could be the cause, consider looking at the next page. It will provide you with a comprehensive listing of the most effective actions and techniques to help treat OCD.

Chapter 4: How is Obsessive-Compulsive Disorder be diagnosed?

As we said, many sufferers of OCD recognize that they have a specific kind of behavior that can not be considered to be unusual. The only way to confirm this is conducting an exam that is legitimate. Diagnosis regarding obsessive-compulsiveness may be performed by a psychologist, clinical social worker, psychiatrist, or any other licensed health professional specializing in mental health. As per the Diagnostic and Statistical Manual of Mental Disorders (DSM), those suffering from OCD is believed to be suffering from obsession, compulsion, or both. Obsessions are defined to be ongoing and continuous thoughts or ideas they are described as troubling. They can cause a dramatic increase in anxiety or distress. They also possess the characteristics of being outside the normal range of issues. This can depend on the particular situation of the person. You could also attempt to stop these thoughts and attempt to eliminate them from their minds by taking out the thoughts with a particular action (hence the external manifestations of the situation) and then accept the thoughts for what they truly are.

Compulsions are important in a psychological sense , when they prompt a person perform them in order in order to satisfy an urge. In addition, they follow rigid rules that makes the sufferer feel anxiety for the person suffering. A lot of people who don't suffer from OCD can exhibit the typical behaviors characteristic of this disorder (such in performing an act that is based on a particular pattern or norm) Someone with OCD is distinguished from others by their capacity to feel overwhelmed when they fail to comply with these rules and therefore, they are required to follow these guidelines. If they are able to adhere to these rules, they're required to reduce the strain on their mental stress levels or to prevent something from occurring , even though they're not directly linked to any "untoward" event in any manner.

After that obsessive or compulsive behavior (or both) can take up a lot of time. They can also lead to any kind of academic, social and occupational limitations. Before treatment, and even when the patient receives treatment or similar, it's crucial that the degree of OCD be thoroughly understood. Rating scales are a good alternative to the Yale-Brown OCS. This could facilitate more efficient and effective consultation with psychiatrists.

Differential Diagnostic

Additionally to OCD In addition, there is an identical but distinct OCD and OCD that is the reason it's not surprising that the two disorders are frequently misunderstood. The first is a form of disorder that's not compatible with the person's self-conception. This is why they cause a certain type of anxiety due to the fact that they could erode a person's self-esteem. But, OCPD is a type of disorder that improves the self-image and self-esteem of the person and gives him the perception that it is normal or acceptable.

In the end, OCPD means that the person is unable to determine whether the behavior is no longer sensible since they typically get satisfaction or pleasure from getting in these activities.

It is also essential to distinguish OCD with other addictions, such as excessive drinking or eating out. The majority of the time they are fun however, OCD activities don't.

What are the ways to get OCD be treated for?

Obsessive-Compulsive disorders are typically linked with stigmatization in the society and also stigmatization of people who suffer. Although those who suffer recognize that there is a problem however, they're not able to seek for help with the mental wellbeing of their patients. Some are seeking help, but they cannot find any relief or "cure" from specific methods of treatment. There is an explanation for this. It is that an issue with the American Psychiatric Association has noted that certain therapies (psychoanalysis and psychotherapy that is dynamic specifically) aren't able to show tangible improvements when controlled.

There are options, however, which may ease OCD symptoms. OCD. This can be achieved by using cognitive behavior therapy, also known as behavioral therapy and specific medications.

Behavioral Therapy

There's a specific treatment method which can aid in overcoming OCD symptoms. OCD known as exposure or Ritual Prevention ERP, or ERP. It's an illustration of exposure therapy.

The approach is based on the belief that therapeutic effects can be obtained by allowing patients to face their fears, thus decreasing their escape reactions. This kind of reaction is known as the Pavlovian response, which is also called the respondent's path to death.

An excellent illustration can be found for people whose OCD manifests as an anxiety that they may contact "contaminated" objects. It is possible to touch an object that been in contact with something is considered by the person to be "contaminated" (such things like objects discovered in the vicinity of streets). This is known as what's known as the "exposure" part. Normal response is to immediately wash their hands , which is the event of an obligation. It is best to avoid this until the person has the ability to adjust to the surrounding. This could lead to lessening the anxiety levels of the person, and also allowing the person to touch the sample which is significantly "contaminated" when compared to the original sample.

This type of ERP has been proven to be very effective in reducing anxiety, which is the characteristic of OCD. It is generally considered as one of the most effective treatments. However, it is not without its critics due the fact that some research studies carried out on it have revealed some doubts about its reliability.

Medicines

There are also certain medications that are prescribed to people suffering from OCD generally to correct any hormonal imbalances that may be the root of the issue. As we mentioned earlier one of these medications is SSRIs , also known as Selective Serotonin Release Inhibitors. Tricyclic antidepressants (such such as Clomipramine) can also be used.

In the field that of OCD It is the need to increase the dosages to subscribing, which are in use. Many other drugs, such as benzodiazepines have been found to be being prescribed however they do not have any evidence that supports their effectiveness.

There are also other medications that are classified as antipsychotics which are atypical (such as quetiapine) which have been found to be beneficial when used in conjunction with SSRIs. They are typically used to treat cases of OCD that are classified by the therapy therapist as "treatment resistant". However, they can cause negative metabolic impacts that can make their use less effective. In addition, none of these substances have been proved to be efficient when used in the absence of any other substance.

Electroconvulsive therapy

In extreme circumstances in the context of OCD, ECT or electroconvulsive therapy has been proven to be extremely efficient. It is sometimes described as "shock treatment" since it is a typical treatment where electroconvulsive seizures are given to patients in order to provide relief from mental illness. However, ECT is rarely used by itself, as it's usually used in conjunction with other treatments.

Many people are conscious of this method to deal with the symptoms of catatonia manic depression, schizophrenia, and major depression disorders. It is often portrayed in various media outlets as a painful experience. However, in actual fact, ECT is administered in conjunction with an anesthetic agent or an anti-inflammatory drug.

Psychosurgery

In extreme circumstances one of the treatment options listed above may not help in relieving symptoms that are associated with OCD. It is currently possible for patients to undergo psychosurgery. It is regarded as a as a last resort. In this method, the surgery is performed on one specific area of the brain (called the Cingulate Cortex). In a study carried out regarding this procedure, approximately 30% of patients showed improvement after the procedure.

In addition deep brain stimulation and vagus neuro stimulation are the other options to pick since they don't require an organ of the brain. Deep-brain stimulation happens when a device known as"brain pacemaker "brain pacemaker" is placed in the brain and transmits electrical signals to particular areas of the brain through electrodes. It is a well-known method of treating other resistant to treatment diseases such as Essential Tremors Parkinson's Disease as well as chronic pain. The stimulation of the vagus nerve , on the contrary is a very popular treatment for severe depression and epilepsy. It involves surgical placement of a stimulator and stimulating the nerve by the transcutaneous technique.

OCD in children

Therapy has been shown to be an effective method to curb OCD-related rituals for children with the disorder. The most important thing to take into consideration is the involvement of family members especially through observations of behavior and reports. Families are expected to provide positive encouragement for children who are in a position to develop alternatives to the demands. After about a years of therapy, the child needs to comprehend what is causing the urge and devise necessary strategies to handle. After this, the child is growing closer to having more friends, as well as showing a more confident personality and showing more faith in him.

It is also important to keep in mind that, especially for children, experiences of stress like the loss of a loved one in the family loved by the family or bullying can significantly impact the development of OCD. Being aware of these triggers will significantly increase the likelihood of the success of treatment.

Chapter 5: The Ocd isn't an impairment. It's an advantage

The term, "obsessive compulsive disorder" is a term often wrongly understood. Before I tell you the best way to conquer your OCD or help people who suffer with OCD I'd love to give those who are suffering from OCD four points. OCD isn't.

1. OCD cannot be a Synonym for Clean Freak or any other

OCD is now a word that translates to "uptight." However, OCD isn't the only one with this meaning. Think about the times you've said somebody was schizophrenic, bipolar, and you're only talking about someone who is moody. Imagine using the term "cancer" in this manner. A mental illness could be extremely damaging for the sufferer of it, and their loved ones. It can cause disruption to their lives, hamper their ambitions, and create dramatic changes.

2. OCD is not an option.

Compulsive or obsessive behavior is not necessarily a sign of mental illness. Everyone is obsessed with , whether it's playing the date you had last night or your job interview from yesterday in your head or writing the exact identical paragraph to ensure that your essay is written correctly or scrutinizing every aspect for clues about what your peers considered of your character...

But someone who has OCD can't be in a position to "snap off from it." The brain of those suffering from OCD are prone to function differently in these circumstances. It's as if they're "stuck" in the thoughts. Then, the thoughts cause an extreme fear , which causes individuals to develop the habit of compulsive behavior. Compulsion is their only escape.

A OCD sufferer isn't required to clean their bathroom, since they enjoy keeping it clean and tidy. Instead, they're filled with anxiety and worry of what might happen in the event that they do not take good care for their bathrooms.

Even if you don't have OCD You can imagine being so completely consumed by something you're unable to think about anything else until made sure that you'd achieve the result you wanted. You are so consumed by the thoughts of your mind and worry that you're incapable of going to work, meet friends or leave home. Your mind is racing and you're totally obsessed by that one thing.

It's possible that you are at a loss, but that's part that defines who you really are.. If you're not in the right place regardless of how hard it may be, it's still possible to be at a where you're not feeling the overwhelming anxiety. I'll discuss how to achieve this in Chapter 4.

3. OCD isn't a joke.

No matter how severe OCD is, many do not get help because of the stigma that comes with mental disease. Many are scared to speak about it and seek treatment, and they are ashamed that they are lacking. Certain studies have shown that just one out of three people suffering from obsessive-compulsive disorder will tell their physician about the symptoms. What's the reason why that it is acceptable in the field of medicine to fight the disease like cancer but not an illness that affects the mind? What causes a problem with the brain less significant than a disease that affects the whole body?

However, making the issue of mental illness a subject of ridicule is an essential part of the issue. It propagates the idea that OCD is something that one can overcome. It suggests that anyone who isn't able to overcome it is naturally weak. People are able to cover up their illness from their family and friends, instead of acknowledging the condition and reaping massive advantages.

The fact is, OCD is treatable. Certain people can be helped with therapies and medication, while others may benefit from making the necessary steps to transform their thoughts of obsession into a catalyst for change. In the real world, it is possible to conquer OCD and live a healthy and fulfilled life.

4. OCD isn't a Quirk.

Imagine this scenario: you're at school and have a roommate. Your roommate has a large quantity of textbooks on the bookshelf you have to share. Instead of arranging her books by author or subject , her suggestion is to organize according to the hues of the rainbow.

Do you believe this is a feasible index system? It's not really. But it can make your roommate smile. Also, it makes her laugh. It doesn't mean she's OCD. The books she was using to study weren't arranged according to the order of rainbow because she believed that it was necessary for easing an anxiety-related trance. The reason she liked pretty colors is that she simply loves pretty colors.

Let me serve as an example. I have a few items about kitchen sponges. I have one for washing dishes and one to clean my countertops in my home. I'm irritated when family members of mine make use of the wrong sponge in the wrong way. This irritates me, and I'm not a proponent of germs. It's not OCD as well.

If I find that someone is using the incorrect sponge, I'll take it off and buy another one. I will consider the issue resolved. For those who suffer from obsessive-compulsive there's no "problem solved" day for those who suffer from it. When OCD is activated, they have to adhere to a detailed procedure in order to correct the error made. The routines they follow are not a way to indulge. The OCD sufferer isn't washing the countertop 50 times just to have fun. It's due to a constant fear of what could happen in the event that they don't cleanse this area at least fifty times. There is a possibility that they could get sick or transmit the virus on to a loved one, since they cooked their dinner in a space "full with bacteria." But, they're aware that this isn't the case.

Have you ever allowed your mind to be drawn to the most likely scenario that could happen in a specific situation? Imaginethat, for example, that you had to wait on an express train in an afternoon? Imagine sitting in the exact same location for a long period of period of time, while playing the various scenes from Lord of the Flies with the passengers. The doomsday type of thinking is exactly what someone with OCD experiences. It is said that the brains of OCD can't not resist the need to dive into the darkest depths, and the darkest, regardless of the situation they find themselves in. It's certainly not a trend. For those who are an OCD patient this is a form of torture.

OCD is not a matter of logic. It's all about anxiety and, if you have the right thought patterns, anxiety can be managed.

OCD is an advantage . is not a disability

I went to a class on OCD. After everyone was done talking about their problems one person asked about OCD and workplace ethics. The host actually laughed and said she believes that the OCD employees are among the most productive ones she's had. I laughed too, but it's true!

OCD can impact a person's performance, and other aspects of their life. However, this is an advantage. As I've mentioned, OCD is not something that one can choose to suffer from just like all of us have our own natural characteristics. So although some people aren't yet aware of the potential of OCD I'm here to demonstrate that no reason to worry about it, however difficult, that doesn't have to be. It's not even good. This is what happens to most OCD sufferers:

It's okay to admit when you're not right. Once you've learned to manage your OCD when it causes confusion in your daily life,, you'll be in control of the annoying thoughts that result from it. If you are unable to manage the thoughts, you'll know and be able recognize when it's essential.

You have a tremendous dedication to your job. If you work in a position which requires you to check items for accuracy, you're bound to become an expert in this field. Additionally, these kinds of examinations will teach you to be alert and give you every each day practice of understanding the difference between what's acceptable and what isn't. In addition, OCD sufferers often have an ambition to do their best in all the activities they participate in and that is a great thing at work.

You look at things that others aren't. If it's related to others or an issue that you are trying to address then you'll be thinking differently, do you not? Many OCD sufferers have an emotional connection that isn't apparent to everyone else.

Do you have similar compulsions or obsessions? If one of your greatest desires is to be concerned about the emotions of other people You must be able to take care of them with love. Be a good example to strangers. Are you worried that your ideas aren't in of the same place? It is best to look for a work that can accommodate your creativity.

If you're struggling to find the other facet associated with OCD I'm going to give you this challenge: contemplate the ways that OCD has transformed you to who you're today. What do you believe OCD has done to you?

If you're considering this, let me introduce five people suffering from OCD who have made it a the success they have achieved in their. Professions.

Chapter 6: The Common Obsessions of Ocd

The anxiety of being exposed to infection, contamination and germs

Based on research in the field of medicine, OCD is a kind of mental disorder where sufferers are plagued by repeated thoughts, thoughts ideas, obsessions, and thoughts that lead them to commit mistakes in their desire. The affliction can affect daily life and can cause interruption to the person's work as also their personal and family life. Italso causes a lot of amount of pain and suffering for the patient as well as his family. Heart rate rises when these thoughts are lingering in their mind. In this state, the patient is contemplating and believes it's an indication that the injury has already begun and that urgent intervention needs to be taken. If the mind is in a anxiety state, the body is stressed and the person decides to do something (like washing or cleaning) to reduce the fear. The person who observes it may seem normal, however the person struggling is trying to alleviate the stress and does the act. There is always a fear of infection bacteria, germs and contamination because the majority of people are meticulous and cautious by nature. They wash their hands every often with soap, and it will appear normal to you.

While there is pollution everywhere , and it's not healthy eating food with no washing your hands or cleaning them and taking it to the level of obsession because of extreme anxiety and stress could be classified as an illness. Hand washing was discussed in detail in the play by Shakespeare in the"Macbeth" Macbeth'. Lady Macbeth had a plan to murder the

King, and also hiring Duncan to kill Duncan. She would always wash her hands, as she was scared that blood would drip from the surface. The fear and anxiety that she felt resulted in her becoming an obsessive character within the production. The washing of hands is a regular practice known as the "LadyMacbeth Effect". To keep their hygiene in check People take things to extremes which can be described as an obsession.

Verifying the door locks, lighting , and electrical appliances

Most people are scared of being struck by electricity or robbed. They make sure their locks are secure and switch off all appliances that require electricity and inspect their doors regularly. This isn't because they're scared. They fear damage, crime, or theft to themselves. Be aware that these thoughts are unwelcome, repeated thoughts that can only add stress. Simply looking at the light won't help decrease the anxiety. In fact, it will increase the terror. The more you check at your back, the more unsecure you feel. You think you're secure by looking every now and then. But what you're actually thinking about are unidentified threats. This anxiety increases every day. Your anxiety is the cause of your fear and the constant constantly checking. Once you've rid yourself of anxiety, the need to keep checking will go away instantly.

The best method to face this fear is to confront it. The idea of a fictional burglar has to be removed from the mind. In this case the medication will not be sufficient to alleviate the problem. Therapy sessions and counseling can help in reducing anxiety. Meditation can help to calm the anxious mind and aid in creating positive mental images.

Serotonin Reuptake could be utilized as a treatment option for OCD. Serotonin is a chemical released by the brain that aids cells in communicating with each other. Serotonin reuptake medication can inhibit serotonin's absorption by the brain, and let more serotonin to be available. This keeps the patient relaxed and happy.

Concerned about the righteousness of other people

There is a notion that the disorder is a genetic disorder. It's possible that you're currently suffering from the disorder, but it may show up later in your life. There has to be a reason for you to be affected by this disorder. Trauma, stress, or illness could trigger OCD however, you have to be genetically predisposed to the condition.

OCD can also be genetic. If a parent or close family member suffers from OCD or other bipolar or anxiety disorders it is likely to develop OCD at some point throughout your life. It is more likely to happen in the case of these sufferers. People who have been in the military or defense forces, or worked as either an attorney or judge within a law-making authorities are thought of as moral beings and the signs of OCD could manifest into these people when there is an existing disorder.

In their efforts to enforce the law they violate the law. Their pride makes them be extremely concerned about the smallest errors that happen in their environment. Being constantly blamed by loved ones for small mistakes makes them an inconvenience as well as makes them feel disregarded by their families and loved ones. They adhere to their own rules and regulations over others. They are so strict that they are the source of their own.

Subcortical and frontal brain structure appear distinct from the normal people. It isn't known whether there's a connection between OCD and disorders in particular brain regions. Researchers are studying this subject. If they can determine the root cause, treatment becomes simple.

A fascination with the thought about sexuality

Vinnie was 13 when she was content playing with her cat at school. One day, her cat hit her boob with a hand and Vinnie was stunned. Vinnie was puzzled and had the cat rub her boob for a second time. The reaction was the same and she was astonished again. She was terrified after the incident. She was anxious about telling her mother about the incident. What if she was sceptical? She thought about sharing the details to her classmates at school. However, she was afraid of being called a'slut' by them. Vinnie was having the sexual urges and starting to sexually assault. At the beginning, she wasn't thinking about it. However, later on, when she imagined falling in a relationship with a snake, she was terrified to death of. Each when the snake was spotted, she was tempted to get in touch with your intimate parts. She wasn't certain who she should talk to and was scared.

Vinnie was embarrassed as she was different to other girlsand they she was ridiculed for her choice. Vinnie felt a sense anxiety whenever she imagined "making things happen" by sexually engaging with children. Her imagination was wild and she was elated and eager to rid herself of the anxiety that she felt sexual. If she thought about her thoughts, she'd stand up and shake her head. She then got drunk, sweaty and covered in terror.

Vinnie was always thinking about sexual matters and this affected her. At school, she washed every person who came into her environment including youngsters. She was in a rush to kiss their intimate areas and went as that she got in the bathroom of junior boys. In fear, she fled the room. She sought refuge via the internet. She watched porn for kids and fell in love. Vinnie was unable to concentrate on her studies and her grades fell. Her mother was unaware of her anxieties. When school officials demanded her mother be responsible for her poor academic achievement, Vinnie's mom spoke directly to Vinnie about the matter. But, Vinnie was in a sexually-driven world of her own, and was living in fear and terror. In the hopes of discovering the reason behind Vinnie her mother took her to visit the school counselor. Vinnie did not share with her any of her fantasies or desires and nothing was to be gained from it.

As time passed, Vinnie became a gorgeous 16-year-old. On her first date with her boyfriend she was engaged in sexual sex while in the trance state, and the man was astonished by her behavior. It was widely believed by guys who thought Vinnie was a sexually attractive siren. A majority of men were keen to make contact with her. Vinnie had a sexual encounter with five guys in just a month, and was not happy. She contacted guys online on dating sites and was enthralled being with them on the camera on the internet. Her interest grew each day, and so did her anxiety.

Following an accidental meeting the friend of hers visited Vinnie's phone and was shocked to find naked pictures of children on her photos gallery. Confused by the revelation the girl shared it with a few other acquaintances, and they confronted Vinnie. Uncertain of the appropriate words to use or how she should take, Vinnie started to cry and began to recount her thoughts and fantasies. The girls contacted their parents when they observed Vinnie's behaviour was odd and bizarre. The girls' mothers who were psychiatrists, spoke with Vinnie's mom , and then had a meeting with Vinnie to talk about her concerns. She suggested that Vinnie take a poll and then observed the patterns of her thoughts. She after talking to her and observing her behavior, she concluded the fact that Vinnie suffered from OCD. Vinnie's biggest problem was her fear of sexual intimacy. She was of the belief that the more sex she was afraid of, the more likely it would disappear. The more sexually attractive that she became, her scared she became a factor.

The best way to deal with Vinnie was to recognize that her thoughts were normal and that meant there was no reason to avoid or dispel them. Sexually obsessive behavior around an age as young as 16 isn't typical and isn't uncommon. Vinnie was advised to recognize her behavior, and not hide from the issue. Vinnie got serotonin to ease her anxiety. The agitation was reduced with medication and sessions with an expert counselor. Vinnie's wild fantasies have stopped along with her obsession for sexual sex.

The obsession with religion and the thoughts of Blasphemy

There's a belief that religion's the primary source of opium for the majority'. Since opium is addictive, religious beliefs and ideas that are not blasphemous are also addictive. The terrorists are instructed to be blasphemous to be able to kill to promote the religion. But that doesn't mean they're being affected by OCD. They've been brainwashed and taught to make choices in a psychotic way. The religion and the religious practices are what drive people to be obsessed and indulgence. Religious people tend to be obsessed with the sermons and religion. They also have the experience of hearing the voices of others and experience hallucinations.

Cleaning, praying, and washing away sins are some of the actions undertaken by OCD patients suffering from OCD. It is interesting to note that some Protestant preachers have signs of OCD. The individuals suffering from OCD are prone to a lot of anxiety regarding their religion, and must adhere to the rituals. If they do not worry about making mistakes and guilt. The other reason for this is they're God fearful and do not consider themselves a God lover. Certain religions have gods that are brutal, meaning that they will be punished if they don't follow their customs in a correct manner. This creates an anxiety in the mind of individuals and makes them feel pressured to follow these rituals. In other words, they fear that they could be placed in Hell.

Violent thoughts

Acute OCD is the kind of disorder that causes violent thoughts within the patient. People suffering from OCD who are suffering from harm OCD are more likely to dream of shooting other people or not wanting to kill anyone using a knife, or any other sharp object, or to remove someone from a structure. Though they never do any of these things however, their thoughts of terror could be disturbing for the sufferer. They imagine assaulting children or self-harming, by throwing themselves into a train or automobile. They avoid areas where they fear that they may be involved in the crime. The terror in their minds from these violent thoughts leads them to withdraw from certain areas and people. However, the trauma still residing in the brain.

Certain therapists are able to make life more difficult for OCD sufferers in their existence by putting them in the subject of. If an OCD sufferer expressed fears of strangling his son, her doctor directed childcare professionals to take away this child as well as the sufferer. This caused more stress for the person who was suffering. Unfortunately, these kinds of people remain a element of society. Support groups are an excellent option for those who suffer from OCD. When they hear similar stories from others they realize that they're not the sole one and that the stories are simply thoughts and not actual happenings. This helps them feel more secure.

The symptoms listed above are common signs of OCD. By manipulating their thoughts , the aid of a psychiatrist will help patients decrease anxiety. Treatment and intervention which is timely will assist the patient overcome their anxieties and living an unhindered life.

Chapter 7: Mindful Review

Technique

In the event that you're conscious of some aspects of OCD recovery, you've realized that it's about learning to deal with the fear of uncertainty.

There's a common misconception about what this really signifies. It doesn't mean that we have to believe that the worst can never happen or that we're bound to live in absolute uncertainness at all times.

Let's face it in this situation. In a situation that is uncertain and where the possibility of serious consequences is at stake, being worried about it is normal.

The recovery process from OCD isn't about embracing complete uncertainty. It's not even about certainty either, as the need to be certain through compulsive behavior is the cause of the whole problem of OCD.

It's all about settling for enough certainty.

It's difficult to determine the concept of what "enough" assurance means. At the point where we need to decide if it's enough and set an end-to end objective. I'll go over what this means and the best way to achieve it in the next chapter on how to establish the ultimate goal.

The methodology that is described in this chapter was intended to help you achieve this with enough certainty. In one report it's referred to as Perceptive Experimental Validation. I call it mindful-checking. Simply put, mindful-checking is paying attention to everything that needs to be examined.

It doesn't require physically checking the object. It can be any type of mental check , like reviewing thoughts, evaluating emotions and memories, and the list goes on.

The main thing to remember is that it's only done - there's no need to go over and over in the hopes of establishing absolute certainty. We're satisfied with the level of certainty.

Application

I'm able to recall the thread on a forum I read about someone suffering from OCD who was asking whether he should have a look since he believes his condition is worsening because he's not taking the time to test.

If you're feeling sicker due to the absence of a medical check, ensure that you test! Be aware that the motive behind the actions we're taking is to act in line with our beliefs. We don't want to get unwell. If it's beneficial to us to have a check-up for illnesses, then we must take a look.

We perform things because we would like to, not because we need to.

The way that forum concerns were phrased, it created the seem like he wasn't under control, or had to ask permission to conduct an investigation.

There's a possibility that we believe that it is a requirement however, remember that nothing is intrinsically driven. Compulsions arise by us when we use them as an automatic response when we are stressed, when they don't actually benefit us.

If they help us in the way they do, then the fact that anxiety is present at all isn't important. I'll discuss this more in the section about value extraction. However, basically we're trying to determine the significance of the actions we perform. If there's value through the check process and we perform it, then we should perform the task. If we're confident that there is a need for it or not, or causes us to feel uncomfortable or not , they're not essential.

Let's suppose I get out of the bathroom and am suddenly thinking. "What would happen for me if I don't pour the soap in the right alcove?" This leads me to check because it shouldn't be harmful if I didn't have soap.

Instead of fighting with myself over whether or not I should check for a need or a desire is more important than the option to choose, I'll be aware about what's happening in the moment. I'll be aware of whether soap is present then I'll be done.

I won't go back every timeand doubt whether soap is the bottle or not, since that's why I decided to take it slow for the first time.

Sometimes when the fear is persistent and keeps us from having to examine every time the exact issue, it could be necessary to set an objective to be addressed in the following chapter.

Chapter 8: Treatment of symptoms with A Healthy Lifestyle

A balanced, healthy lifestyle which includes healthy eating habits along with regular exercise and sufficient sleep will help you beat the symptoms of OCD and re-training your brain to function normally. The brain's chemicals are directly affected by the food that you consume. Blood sugar levels can be affected by your diet habits too as your sleep habits, which could influence your OCD symptoms. Exercise can aid your body deal with anxiety that is associated with OCD disorder by focusing your attention away from the negative thoughts and thoughts. Additionally drinking alcohol, smoking and sleep deprivation must be avoided to assist your body to deal with the OCD symptoms better.

Establish Good Eating Habits

1. Eat breakfast, lunch as well as dinner, on a consistent on a regular.

This will help to maintain your blood sugar levels in check and will also help to reduce your cravings for certain foods increase your metabolism, and ensure that you're making the most of your body's capabilities. These are all essential to calm the OCD thoughts and feelings. It is recommended to eat breakfast frequently in addition to dinner and lunch. You can also have small snacks between meals and before you go to sleep.

2. Eat foods that improve your mood

Omega-3 oils and Omega-6. Your overall well-being and mood can greatly improve if you consume sufficient and balanced amounts of omega-3, and omega-6 oil in your daily diet. Omega-3s can be found in cold-water cold-water fish oily , flaxseedsand pumpkin seeds and flaxseeds, hemp, walnuts and hemp. The oils of vegetables (walnut as well as sunflower oil and safflower, flax, sunflower and corn) and soybeans) are high in omega-6 fatty acids.

Tryptophan. Serotonin, a brain-related chemical which regulates mood of an individual, is produced through the amino acid vital to our lives and health, tryptophan. Tryptophan can be found in baked potatoes and oil-rich seafood, nuts as well as legumes and seeds including poultry, seeds, and Oats.

Complex Carbohydrates. Serotonin levels within your brain can be increased by a diet that is an appropriate blend of complex carbohydrates minerals, vitamins, and proteins.

Healthy Snacks. Fruits with yogurt or seeds and raisins and nuts, along with whole meal breads with peanut butter are great examples of healthy snacks.

Exercise Regular

Regular exercise can help relieve the tension and stress associated with your obsessional-compulsive symptoms of the disorder. Your mental and physical health can be improved through regular exercising. Also, your levels of satisfaction will increase because of the release of endorphins within your brain. These are often referred to as feel-good chemicals. To get the most out of any aerobic workout it is advised to train each day for 30 minutes or more. Five examples of great exercises to try include:

1. Walking

Walking is a wonderful form of exercise you can participate in. It's not only easy to complete (as as little as five minutes can have a major impact) and doesn't require any special equipment and can be completed virtually anywhere however it is recommended to do it in a comfortable outdoor environment. It's possible to increase your enjoyment when you walk with your companion or a friend.

2. Swimming

It doesn't matter whether you use gentle or powerful strokes and swimming allows you to submerge your body in water to experience its relaxing and soothing effects. It is advised to go swimming at the time of the day when the pool isn't too crowded You can swim at your own speed that will help you relax and unwind.

3. Yoga or Pilates

Both Yoga and Pilates are non-competitive and safe kinds of exercises that could help improve your mood, increasing how well you sleep and reducing the stress levels you experience.

4. Martial arts

When done in a relaxed manner, you can focus on your breathing, your inner control and mental discipline. It will also assist you in battling negative thoughts and urges.

5. Team sports for teams

Participating in any team sport and especially when it's performed with your close friends can be beneficial for your OCD condition.

Eliminate Alcohol and Nicotine

Although alcohol has been found to reduce anxiety and anxious feelings related to OCD symptoms, the effects are temporary and could trigger anxiety-related feelings to pop out in the future. Similar to cigarettes, they offer some relief. But, as the nicotine they contain is a stimulant cigarettes can cause an increase in levels of anxiety, as well as symptoms of obsessive-compulsive disorder.

Make sure you get enough rest

Lack of sleep can result in more OCD thoughts and feelings. Make sure you are at a the right level of rest to ensure your mental health and to eliminate all OCD symptoms.

Chapter 9: How to Get Ocd Diagnosed. Way Does Ocd Get diagnosed and then confirmed

If you're sure that you have an OCD confirmation has been made it is possible to start treating and managing the disorder. Naturally, the most efficient method of determining the degree of the disorder is to talk to an expert doctor and perform precise laboratory tests. The diagnosis of OCD is confirmed by the following methods.

Diagnostic tests in the laboratory

There are many lab tests that doctors can conduct to rule out other diseases that might produce similar symptoms.

Thyroid function test (TFT)--This test is used to measure the levels of hormones, as well as the levels of Triiodothyroxine in the serum (T3) as well as the test for serum Thyroxine (T4). These hormones are the main hormonal hormones that our body utilizes to regulate metabolism. any variation in their levels could cause a variety of symptoms, such as mental disorders as well as insufficient organs, an irregular menstrual cycle , as well as various other signs that resemble symptoms of OCD.

The normal values for T3 range between 80 to 180 ng/dl (nanograms per deciliter) and T4 ranges from 4.6 at 12 mg/dl (micrograms in one deciliter). Any value that falls lower or higher than the thresholds indicates an issue.

Complete blood count (CBC)--This is the total number of blood cells in your body. This includes White blood cells (WBC) and red blood cells (RBC) and platelets. An increase in WBC could indicate an infection with bacteria or leukemia and other diseases. A decrease in WBC could be a sign that there is leucopenia, viral infections or anemia. An increase in RBC may indicate polycythemia vera and a decrease could indicate anemia.

Screening tests for drugs and alcohol generally involve tests on cards that are used to determine whether someone is taking illegal drugs or an alcohol drinker. The combination of drugs and alcohol can cause people to develop false beliefs or thoughts that can cause them to commit sexually explicit criminal acts , or even horrendous criminal actions. This is because both of these substances alter the brain's functioning. They have the ability to stimulate or block the central nervous system (CNS). Some examples of illegal substances and their effects are:

Cocaine is among the most commonly consumed drug. The active ingredient benzoylecgonine has been recognized to trigger hallucinations as well as feelings of euphoria.

Heroin, and its metabolite Morphine can trigger daydreams. withdrawal symptoms may be accompanied by seizures, as well as cardiac arrest.

Marijuana--Its active component, delta-9 tetrahydrocannabinol, can produce hallucinations and a sense of well-being.

Each of these illicit substances can cause psychological and physical dependence which could lead to more OCD and prevent appropriate treatment.

Physical Exam (PE)

Doctors will carry out an extensive examination on your body in order to discover if there is a physical cause to your symptoms. It is likely that the PE will also detect indicators of OCD such as hand-related injuries and other body parts which resulted from routine washing. Your attire (no hair that's off-color) and how you behave (extremely focused when you speak) will reveal your character weaknesses.

Medical Histories

The question will inquire about your OCD background of your family. Do you have a known medical diagnosis for OCD? If so, you are likely to are suffering from OCD. However, it's not completely certain. experts have noticed that OCD typically occurs within families of the same type.

Psychological evaluation

Psychological tests can be conducted to determine if the symptoms stem from the presence of other mental disorder. These tests can narrow your possibilities and assist in determining if you are suffering from OCD or a different mental illness. The psychiatric center can be contacted to take a test in the event the results aren't clear.

To verify that you're experiencing OCD The following conditions must be met

You are obsessed with one idea , and are inclined to act in a compulsive way.

Your actions demonstrate your passion and determination.

Your cravings and desires are always present, consistent and purposeful.

A majority times you're unaware that you're engaging in compulsive, or obsessive behaviors.

Your actions could create extreme stress and anxiety.

Social life can be affected by these behaviors.

You attempt to regulate your behavior so that it is different but when you fail, you are stressed you feel.

Another way to check is whether you suffer from OCD and OCD as well. If your behavior is consistent with the main requirements, you may want to think about making an appointment with your doctor.

It is crucial to keep in mind that the results of all tests are analyzed in conjunction in order to establish the proper diagnosis. The doctor is accountable to this responsibility. So, it is important to choose your doctor with care.

Chapter 10: Causes of Ocd

Despite the myriad theory and study studies about OCD experts haven't yet found the reason behind the disorder.

There are many theories , however it was thought that the factors that trigger OCD may cause a combination of psychological and hereditary behavior and environmental issues.

Hereditary

There are studies in the field which suggest OCD is an inherited disorder. It is believed that the disorder could be passed through generations from one generation to the next, and later be passed on through generations.

Studies have revealed that 45 to 65 percent of children who suffer from OCD were affected by genetics although the research isn't conclusive. The reason for this is because of the studies of identical twins, there's a lot of cases where one has OCD while the other did not.

It is thought that genetics may have a greater impact on someone has been diagnosed is a child rather than as an adult. It is an unsubstantiated theory since no genes has yet been identified to explain the cause.

Bio

As for genes one gene commonly linked with OCD is hSERT, which is called the gene that regulates human serotonin. This gene is a neurotransmitter, which plays a role in the development of serotonin transporters inside the brain.

The function for the transporter's job is take in serotonin once the nerve cell shares with another nerve that is adjacent to it. If the hSERT functions too fast, the user may suffer from certain symptoms of OCD.

Another gene thought to be responsible for OCD can be found in SLC1A1, called GTP The gene that regulates glutamate. This gene is actually very similar to the hSERT. However , it's like the name implies, capable of taking in glutamate, a different neurotransmitter, instead of serotonin.

Environmental

The influence of various environmental factors are taken into consideration when examining the underlying causes of OCD. Research has revealed that stress in childhood along with the influences of the parents can be among the causes which contribute to the growth of OCD. Between 53 and 73 percent cases are believed to be due to the influence of their environment.

The way in which a child is brought into the home of parents could increase the chance of developing, or even being diagnosed with OCD in the in the near future. Additionally, it is thought that if one is always stressed, the symptoms of OCD are likely to get worse.

Other causes of environmental origin for OCD include issues with relationships and sexual abuse, significant or unplanned life events such as the passing of a loved ones or the diagnosis of a terminal illness.

Cognitive

OCD is believed to be can be caused by psychological disorders that encompass behavioral and cognitive aspects. The cognitive theory is based on how a person's brain interprets troubling thoughts as detrimental or harmful to him.

In the previous part that OCD sufferers are usually plagued by uncomfortable or unwelcome thoughts. These thoughts may be sexually or profane the sense that they are sexually or profane in.

The thoughts trigger him to react in a way that can help in removing them such as singing or the sound of the sound of. If the person believes that these beliefs are real and that they harm him, he'll continue to follow in his thoughts.

Some experts suggest that untrue beliefs about sexuality or religion in childhood may have triggered this type of thinking.

Behavioral

A different aspect in psychology concerns behavior. This is different from the mental belief that compulsions don't arise due to unwelcome thoughts but rather they are caused by the fear of certain items or situations.

One example of this is the fear of being sick from germs. This could cause people who suffers from OCD to clean their hands frequently. The people with OCD tend to revert to avoidance of what causes them fear instead of confronting it directly. This can lead to the usual compulsive behavior.

Chapter 11: Believe System

Let me offer an analogy

Imagine that you are in a village and there's a small mountain in your town, and everyone in the village claims that nobody can climb it. It's not possible. Everyone accepts and believes in the belief that no one can climb the mountain. In the end, it's an unavoidable prediction for all.

The common belief of people in this particular village at the moment would be similar to Nah It's extremely hazardous and dangerous, almost impossible to ascend the mountain. There's the fear in every mind, including yours, and it's false, and is caused by believing in this illusion at first.

One of the most crucial things to consider is to think of the people in your life as negative thinking which constantly tells you that you're incapable of accomplish it and that there's little hope, and making you feel like it's impossible. This isn't the case because it's a fable, just believing it can make it stronger, nothing less.

OCD is similar to OCD.

Let's continue with the tale. After a while you find out that someone has to climb the mountain and is given an evaluation of the community. After this the fear decreases through a conscious or unconscious manner, and even if it is lower than 1%. You start to believe that it's possible. The negative thoughts and fears decrease to a certain extent and your brain receives the evidence that suggests the possibility of. But, a majority people believe that they were fortunate. If you don't believe most of them are, you can rest assured that your brain acquired some evidence to prove that it's possible. (But most important you can do is to believe the facts that prove it's possible, even though it's not a lot.)

Similar to this it is when you notice that for the first time , you are able to feel satisfied in the midst of OCD or enter your normal mode for the first time and you take note of your feelings in a journal. journal(writing down the experience can help make a stronger impression in the brain's mind) In this manner you are communicating with your brain that it's possible to be in the normal zone(just as you felt a little optimistic when you heard that an individual was able to reach the top of the mountain to the summit for the first time inside the village, giving your brain the message that it's possible to climb the mountain). This could bring you a sense of optimism and hope, and, as I said in the past, it might shift between positive and negative optimistic, since you've endured many years of negative thoughts. The trauma could be intense in beginning but, as time passes, the more you get to the normal state of mind and experience an optimistic state as your brain absorbs information, both in a conscious and subconsciously. In the end, your brain's outlook gets better and it is true that it can reach a level that , even if you're predisposed to compulsive thoughts it's not affecting on you since you're in a place in which you're aware within your mind that it's all a scam .

Where was I? The moment you learnt that a man who was able to climb the mountain, you received glimpses of hope. After a few days, you find out that a woman been able to climb the mountain. Now your fears are lessened which gives you more confidence However, there are some people who are less than they were prior to this, who are still preaching that it's not possible but your brain is armed with more evidence.

Afterward, you learnt that even children had been on the mountain. Your fear has diminished than it used to be and your motivation is beginning to expand because your brain is getting more evidence to prove it's feasible. However, there are just a few people who are not convinced (but considerably less compared to the past) and most of the people are more optimistic regarding the possibilities. (i.e. in the instance (i.e. in the context of OCD (i.e. in the case of OCD when you get to an acceptable level and begin to feel more positive about it and anxiety decreases significantly.)

At the summit, you can see different groups of people trying to scale the summit of the hill (in the setting of OCD your optimism has risen even more) It becomes apparent that it was simple , and then you realise that the whole thing was just an illusion of terror it was the negative image that the people put on the villager, and you realise that you don't have to stress, the process that is climbing the mountain isn't too difficult, and at this point you don't have to worry any of the small comments made by the people who are negative and their negative remarks.

Then, you climb the mountain. There might be a bit of fear, but you overcome it.

Similar to the method used to recover from OCD. You can enter to the zone of normality in an enormous manner, and eliminate the bogus assumptions e.g. that relate with OCD in the sense of religion POCD, HOCD specific thoughts OCD and much more. You are aware of its tricks, and has no power anymore and eventually, you have been completely restored. Your anxiety won't be the same.

Another proof of the efficacy of the Belief System comes taken from an actual event:

It was the norm for professional athletes to run distances of one mile (1.6kms) in under four minutes seemed impossible.

The human body can't physically keep up with this pace of speed without falling apart.

For quite a while running, athletes have been fighting time, and the inconceivable four minutes have always beaten them.

It's like a mountain that is that is unbeatable in size. The closer it was to being ascent, the more intimidating it looked.

It was the ultimate aim of sporting excellence.

The 4 minute mile ran for many years, and all the experts concerned believed that in case a person broke it, the break would happen in an exact scenarioof perfect conditions: 20 degrees, with no wind on a particular kind of track: dry hard clay. In an atmosphere of huge crowd who cheered the runner on to the most impressive running performance of his lifetime.

The basic idea is that there ought to be a lot of luck.

...Yet Roger Bannister was able to do it on a cold, cold day, on the wet track of the track's small size in Oxford and in front of a small crowd.

It was not anything more than chance.

At the time he did this, the majority of adversaries were delighted.

"At the end of the day, someone was doing it"

What transpired after Bannister's shattering belief of "running one mile for just four minutes is impossible?"

Yes,

Each dog owner and their dog started running for a mile in under four minutes.

It wasn't due to their speed, fitness or endurance dramatically increased.

The reason for this was that Bannister had granted them release from the mental institution they were in.

The problem involved more of a psychological problem than one that was physical.

Human beings are able to behave according of the beliefs they hold about their lives and the environment in which they live..

If you are able to grasp the idea, it will change your life.

Your belief systems (subconscious mind), LITERALLY HAS THE FUCKING ABILITY TO ALTER BEHAVIOURAL FUNCTIONS IN YOUR PHYSICAL BODY.

If you believe that you're in the right place with your thoughts, you'll only realize that it is if you believe that your thoughts aren't affecting you. thinking (i.e. your thoughts don't affect the way you live) and you're happy regardless of what you think , you'll enjoy the happiness and positivity you deserve.

Your subconscious mind will allow you to assume the character of a fucking guy in the ripe fruit, and shut off your negative thoughts.

Something else I'd like inform you about the belief that your I.Q facial hair, length, body hair, etc. could be genetic. But, remember...

Belief System is never genetic.

It's something you make entirely by yourself.

Everyone can develop their own opinions. Every person has different or less conviction than others.

If you're interested, I've outlined the steps you can follow to build your own beliefs about OCD. It's a process, after all, anyone can master it. So, it is essential to adhere to the guidelines laid out in this guide with complete honesty.

No excuse.

Chapter 12: Controlling The Ocd of Yourself

It can be difficult for those with OCD to seek assistance. Let's look at some ways individuals can use to manage their OCD symptoms on their own.

Take away the trigger. Be aware of the trigger and avoid any thing that could cause your symptoms. For instance, if there is a specific place or image that triggers thoughts of obsession avoid the things that can trigger.

Remove yourself from the location. In some instances, it is best to leave the area that you cannot meet your requirements. For instance, you're compelled to wash your hands after for a long stroll however there isn't a sink to wash your hands in.

Redirect your attention. Sometimes, it's difficult to get up or move. Another option is to shift your focus to another thing or thought. The trick is to choose something that you are excited about in order to distract your attention from your thoughts. Make sure you choose something that is demanding your attention, to ensure that when you're focused on the task, you don't let your mind drift off with your thoughts.

Record it in your diary. Keep a notebook to capture what you think and feel, and later write them down. Writing down your thoughts or needs can help ease anxiety.

Prepare yourself for urges and anticipate them. Avoiding urges before their occurrence can assist you in managing the desire. Make a plan to address the urge. For example, if are aware that you'll have to lock your door ensure that you've done it the right way first time. When you've locked the door, tell yourself "I closed the door." Make a picture within your head of the locked door. After you exit the room, tell yourself "The door is closed" and then think of the mental image. Another method of ensuring that you're completely convinced is to record yourself telling yourself "today is Monday and I've secured my doors." If you're sure you'll be able close the door again, you could play your tape of yourself declaring the date and confirming that you've closed the door.

Allow yourself to be worried. For instance, you can give yourself two times of anxiety, starting in the early morning and another later in the evening. If you be anxious or experience symptoms, set aside the time to worry period. Then , during the time of worry, allow yourself to worry but only for the duration of your worry. The duration and amount of times you worry will vary among individuals depending on how serious your symptoms appear. Once you've established a pattern that you follow, you'll be able to reduce your worrying time. For instance, after one month of worry sessions lasting 15 minutes, you should reduce your worries to 14 minutes.

Try meditation and relaxation techniques. These activities can help reduce anxiety, particularly in a group of people. It's not suitable for everybody, so you should seek out something you are able to relax and enjoy enjoying. For instance, take excursion or stroll in a group or on your own.

Exercise regularly. The benefits of exercise are endless , and working out can ease stress by helping you focus your attention. If you're only beginning an fitness routine, make sure not to do too much. Start with a 30-minute workout and then increase your time to the time is an hour. Aerobic exercise can work almost each muscle you have and increases your heart rate, as well as the capacity of your body to absorb oxygen. Exercise can improve your overall health by production of the hormone endorphins. the brain's hormone which creates a feeling of well-being.

Get a good night's sleep! Make sure you get at least 8 hours of rest each day. If someone is asleep at night the body starts an process to detoxify and repairs. It's the body's attempt to heal any tissues which may be damaged from the day's activities. This is also the time when the organs begin their cleansing process so that the body can be cleansed of toxins and returned to its normal condition. If your body isn't getting enough rest every night, your tissues can't heal themselves, resulting in diseases. Additionally, toxins that are supposed to be removed from the body during rest remain in the body, and can lead to illnesses. Sleeping is an excellent method to lead a healthy and stress-free lifestyle and is a great protection against unwarranted behaviour patterns and thoughts.

Find out what is wrong and seek help. Although OCD is a common problem for a large number of people, a lot of OCD cases aren't recognized. While it is possible to to treat OCD but the best method to manage the condition is seeking out the help of a doctor.

Chapter 13: The Treatment for Ocd

Medication

The first option for treatment and usually the most effective, is medication. 90% of OCD sufferers will benefit from treatment as those in a position to benefit are likely to notice a reduction of 50% in symptoms, provided they follow the prescribed dosages. The most commonly used drugs to treat OCD are popular antidepressants such as Prozac, Paxil, and Zoloft. It's important to remember that every antidepressant has its own unique characteristics and some might not affect OCD symptoms at all , and others can only treat specific types symptoms of OCD symptoms. This is why it's crucial to consult an expert medical doctor prior to beginning any treatment.

Following the treatment plan that your doctor has recommended is crucial. Most

OCD sufferers quit taking their medication at some point due to undesirable negative side effects or other causes.

The inability of taking the medication you are prescribed even for a short period of time could result in an imbalance of the chemical system of your body that may make your symptoms worse. In reality, the most common issues sufferers face while taking antidepressants arise as due to the regularity of their dosage, not an issue of the medicine itself. If you're concerned about negative effects of medication, you'd rather begin with the lowest dose you can, and then gradually increase dosage should you end up have decide to quit taking the medicines completely. Always consult your doctor before you start taking any medication.

Psychological Treatments

The use of medications is effective in reducing the effects of OCD but there is no method to get rid from it completely. A proper approach to improving your health and mental well-being is crucial and crucial for your mental health and to avoid any relapses to compulsive behavior. The most effective treatment methods to treat OCD emphasize the necessity of stopping destructive patterns and behaviors.

When it comes to OCD there are a number of treatments that patients are able to select from, but most concentrate on the basic idea of exposure. Psychologists help patients by exposing them to an object or scenario that he's afraid of, or in a discussions about the origins of their disturbing thoughts and thoughts.

The most well-known type therapy is ERP that stands for treatment for exposure and response. ERP is focused on bringing awareness to the anxiety triggered by your anxieties in tiny amounts, and preventing your from engaging in behaviors that can temporarily reduce anxiety. If you practice this regularly over time, you will notice that the level of anxiety you feel when you are confronted by your fears, it will reduce.

The method is based on the notion conventional conditioning to be the most effective method to utilize. Here's an example of the way it is done.

Mark is an OCD sufferers who is prone to washing his hands each time an object he's thinking of touching is dirty, even if it's just a tiny thing like the doorknob in his house. Mark decides to get treatment by a therapist who specializes in therapy.

The therapist in therapy is able to choose to expose to some harmless dirt. This triggers anxiety. caused, and the patient begins to get anxious. But, the therapist will be able to persuade him to soak his hands in dirt and then clean it with an old towel.

Naturally, this sends Mark into a bizarre state of mind and he makes the decision to leave the room to wash his hands. The therapist suggests that Mark remain in the room . Then, after some help with the patient, he can remain in the room for 10 seconds before washing their hands.

Repeating the process over and over again, the risk of germs that aren't actually present (such as those that are found on the surfaces of your everyday home) will decrease as the person is continually in contact with real bacteria, but without harm the body. In the end, his body and mind are preparing his body and mind for an anxiety response by dealing with his fears. In the near future, he'll be free of his fears completely, but they can be brought on by the most extreme trigger, such as the presence of a very unsanitary condition.

ERP could be accomplished in as short as 20 sessions, but there are programs that are with shorter sessions. Sessions typically last 90 minutes. They involve preparing yourself for the introduction of frightening stimulus, the introduction, and the subsequent handling. While the majority of therapists adopt the method of slowly introducing to the topic or the event during the session, some are quick to introduce the most frightening stimuli (known within the discipline as "flooding" over the issue) to reduce the patient's sensitivity to future sessions. The practice is gradually losing because it could result in the patient to not show up for future sessions.

Although the majority of people who go to therapy will benefit from it, they also face dangers. Particularly, since the therapy is focused on confronting your fears so it's not a surprise that a large percentage of patients quit the therapy before the conclusion of their therapy. This can be extremely detrimental to the development of the OCD patient and should be avoid at all costs. Even those who attend each session are able to skip having to complete what they call "homework" they are required to finish, which is a set of mental exercises or assignments that they receive from their therapy.

While ERP is best suited to people with compulsions, it's also a useful tool for those who are obsessed.

The prevention of a response and exposure may require a considerable amount of time but. This is why it is that it is crucial to have an insurance policy that will cover psychological problems and physical illnesses since treatment without it could be very difficult for many.

Cognitive Therapy treating your Compulsions at the source

The foundation of cognitive therapy rests on an underlying concept that is , that constant distraction or deformed thoughts cause an inexplicably intense fascination. Many people are plagued by troublesome thoughts, typically daily. However they quickly disappear and then erased.

If you are suffering of OCD In the event that you have OCD You are more likely to think about your thoughts as seriously. For instance, you might you think that your thought could be a sign of what is to come in the past, or that thinking of an event which is tragic could make the incident more likely. This can lead to the situation where a small idea is questioned instead of being ignored, that can lead to a lot of suffering.

If you or an OCD sufferer is unable to stop thinking about the worrying idea, they may turn to compulsions to get rid of their thoughts. This is because anxiety impedes the ability to consider the issue and then dismiss it.

OCD sufferers can also be prone to underestimate the extent to which their thoughts can have on a situation. In this case, for instance, you could be enticed by the need to track the cars passing through your vehicle to prevent falling into the air. Naturally counting cars and preventing the possibility of a crash isn't linked however, counting cars could make you feel more in control of what you believe is not your responsibility.

Cognitive therapy is focused on looking into your thoughts about negative things in depth so that your professional will know the way you think. This is vital since the majority of OCD sufferers get so engrossed in their illness that they aren't aware the distorted thought patterns that they can generate. By highlighting the mistakes and examining different ways of thinking and think, you can enhance the patient's metacognition, and make them less naive and better equipped to make well-informed decisions.

Cognitive therapy is similar to ERP in that it's carried out in an ongoing series of between 10 sessions. Like ERP you'll receive tasks to complete when you return home, and during the course of your day. It could be a matter of keeping a journal of your thoughts, recording when you are stressed and tracking your routine throughout the day. This helps your therapist understand better the illness you suffer from.

Before beginning psychotherapy, it's recommended to look over the following questions and then think long and hard about the answers.

Can I afford to afford it? or will my insurance pay for it?

Do I have the time to commit my time to weekly sessions that could last for six months? Furthermore, I can complete the tasks that my therapist assigns me?

Can I face those things I am scared of the most?

The people who experience the greatest results through psychotherapy are people who are most excited about making a change in their lives and will be committed to sessions of psychotherapy. Before starting the process, you should consult with a variety of therapists to choose one you are at ease with. If you're honest, sincere and honest when you meet with the therapist that you select and you'll soon be on the right direction for healing!

Chapter 14: Prevention of Ocd

Self-care is an essential element in any treatment. It is comprised of five fundamental components that include a healthy diet and exercise routine and restful sleep, as well as relaxation, and the avoiding of harmful behavior. Although it's not going to solve the entire issue however, it can dramatically reduce or stop negative emotions. It can also increase optimism.

Balanced Diet

The importance of eating an proper diet has been made clear many times. Inability to eat food for longer periods of time may cause anxiety, which is why it is suggested to consume smaller meals with short breaks.

Carbohydrates are the most important source of energy for OCD. They not only calm the person however, they also increase serotonin levels too. However, the excessive consumption of these substances could cause different medical issues therefore only the proper amount of carbohydrates is required.

Regular Exercise

An exercise routine of 30 minutes every day can provide numerous advantages. You will feel more calm and less stressed because of the release of endorphins. It's also a great distraction in the event of obsessive thoughts or routine behavior. Other advantages include a healthier body, and less sensitive to various ailments.

Get enough sleep

Sleeping problems may be due to anxiety. Lack of sleep can trigger the anxiety to increase. However , getting the right amount of sleep can lead to the mental health of your child.

There are a variety of ways to help the OCD sufferer sleep well. A relaxing music playlist or a clean room can provide the perfect environment to relax. Eye fatigue can help you sleep better , however watching too much TV that strains your eyes can be detrimental to your health. The best method is to work on relaxation techniques.

Relaxation

A 30 minute daytime routine of relaxation could be beneficial. Alongside helping to get enough sleep, it helps to alleviate anxiety. Stress isn't the sole cause of obsessive-compulsive disorder but it may be the trigger for the development of the disorder. It can also result in complications with the symptoms of the disorder.

There are numerous techniques for relaxation that you can attempt. Yoga of all sorts is one of the most popular alternatives for the wealthy. Alongside the many benefits of yoga, massages are not only cleansing, but equally relaxing. Certain forms of healing art (aromatherapy and sound therapy , regression from past lives, PLR, as well as Hypnotherapy) appear to have advantages in relieving anxiety and stress.

Not all relaxation techniques entail costs. Breathing exercises, for example , are not expensive. In fact, breathing deeply is the main method of relaxation. Another breathing method involves counting tens at a time when you breathe out and exhale. Meditation and self-hypnosis are other forms of free relaxation techniques.

Avoiding Unhealthy Habits

Certain OCD sufferers might experience relief from alcohol, cigarettes and other drugs that are illegal However, the relief may only last for a short time. Alongside the short time of relief, it could cause health problems, which can result in a higher stress level for the sufferers. An addiction to these substances has been identified as being directly related to an increasing frequency of obsessive thoughts and compulsive behaviours.

Despite the advantages of a healthy and balanced lifestyle for treating OCD However, it's important to tackle the obsessional thoughts that accompany compulsive behavior. With a strong support system, fighting OCD symptoms will be much less difficult.

Chapter 15: How to do to manage Obsessive Compulsive Disorder?

Are you constantly checking whether your plan is completed that your lighting is switched off, and your gates are secured? Are you continually annoyed by insidious, destructive thoughts that you have to be able to control with your own personal routine? This article was created to help you cope with Obsessive compulsive disorder (OCD).

Steps

1. Do you know if your issue has been diagnosed medically correct. If you're reading this but aren't sure that you've been diagnosed with clinical OCD or you have strong belief that you might be suffering from OCD. See a doctor to have your condition evaluated by a clinical examination. OCD could be a factor in your

condition. OCD If you show any of the symptoms below:

The habit of looking at everything repeatedly. It could be as simple as making sure that you've shut your door to your car several times, turning the light off and back on at a particular time to determine if they're actually off, or reciting things over and over. People who suffer from OCD generally acknowledge that their behaviors aren't justifiable.

The resemblance is to hand washing or dirt. The affected people wash their hands and arms after coming into contact with something they believe could be "contaminated".

• Intrusive thought patterns. A lot of people with OCD are plagued by intrusive thoughts or thoughts which aren't acceptable and cause anxiety for the sufferer. They typically fall under three categories of violent and inappropriate ideas or sexually offensive thoughts and religious beliefs that are not orthodox.

* A real draw. People are attracted by the process itself. It could be linked to thoughts that are intrusive however, it is not always in those the sense of a specific aspect. It's also likely to connect to anxiety disorders and may be related to a specific problem.

2. Comprehend the obsession/stress/compulsion design. The typical treatment plan used by OCD patients is generally:

"The attraction. The reason is because they believe you're suffering from or have a sly belief and that you are in the "need" to examine everything in your life a number of times.

* The pressure. The attraction could make you feel a lot of tension. If the desire you're seeking is based on a "need" to ensure whether your door is closed 10 times, your stress is due to the fear that you may be taken hostage if the door isn't locked. If you're prone to washing your hands frequently and are concerned about pollutants or germs, it can cause you to feel stressed. Additionally, if you have indecent beliefs or religious beliefs that are defamatory and/or a history of sexual harassment, it could be the result of the fear of being punished.

* Coercion. Coercion is the "routine" that you need to follow to manage the tension created through the pull. It could include checking that the lights have been turned off 5 times praying to yourself or even washing your hands.

3. Learn to remove the pattern. To be able to manage obsessive compulsive disorder, you need to comprehend to avoid the obsession/stress/compulsion pattern from going on.

Take note that the needs aren't in your hands. Whatever you do, you will experience the attraction, be it an assortment of thoughts that are unsettling or a constant confirmation of an idea or the desire to wash your hands or wash your arms. The attraction will be there. It's impossible to do anything about it.

Be aware that the stress is in your control. Your attraction may cause anxiety when you believe that your attraction is justifiable. If you believe you have OCD is the cause of your attraction, you won't be concerned about it. If you suddenly get the need to determine the amount of tiles you have placed on your floor you could declare "I have OCD and it's unhealthful keeping track of the the tiles, so I'm not going to take note of those tiles." The urge to count tiles is an invasion of religious belief that is blasphemous and infuriating. The anxiety you feel could be triggered by the idea the thought that your actions will be stigmatized. If you think your thoughts are caused by OCD then you're not an individual who requires anxiety. The higher power (or whatever you think to be the reality) doesn't penalize people who are afflicted with thoughts that stem from mental disorders that result from control.

Keep in mind that even if it isn't possible to control your pressures, you're capable of stopping yourself from using coercion. Don't do it. Imagine you are to wash your arms constantly. If you are able to learn to not wash your arms quickly and you'll have the ability to stop your habit at the end of the first stage. This can lead to a type commonly referred to as "exposure therapy" that is where patients are "exposed" to a want, but is not permitted to use coercion. Numerous studies conducted in the last 15 years have proved to be true the Cognitive Behavioral Therapy is better than other forms of therapy for OCD. As time goes by the treatment process will become easier and easy.

4. You have to be able to force yourself to think about the issue. This is a great way to reduce a specific anxiety or fear. If you're constantly thinking regarding it, this can result in you becoming insensitive to the circumstances. The reason we stress is because we associate the issue with a negative sensation or experience. If you can turn the negative experience into an enjoyable incident will stop causing you to be worried.

5. Do not let OCD define who you are. You're more than your circumstances. Create a list of all your incredible features and go through it whenever you're having an unlucky day. There will be days of struggle but you must keep going.

6. Enhance Your Performance. Each time you accomplish something or achieve the aim of a new goal Be sure to congratulate yourself. Make a note of your achievements. Spend time with those who are positive , and meet an old friend or a family member. Visit an older person and discuss about the issues. They're more likely to be an attentive listeners.

7. See a specialist. If you are unable to control your illness and it causes problems in your social or your daily routine it is recommended that you seek out a doctor. There is a possibility of receiving

prescribed medications or treatments to alleviate the symptoms.

8. If OCD is causing you to be involved in routines, learn what you can do to manage your behavior. Certain compulsive behaviors can be managed using the methods described in this book , or with guidance by a psychotherapist.

Chapter 16: Initial Treatment: Strategies to Reduce the Symptoms and Effects Ocd Yourself

OCD is a condition that affects a lot of people. Although many movies and TV shows focus on the issues that come with OCD however for those who suffer with it, the issue is much more serious and something that is not funny. OCD can be as serious in its impact on the daily routine of a person since there are specific steps that they need to take in order to decrease anxiety. There are times when patients suffer anxiety attacks. They might experience psychotic episodes in the event that they are unable to perform the same routine.

Before any medication or treatment can be effective, it's vital that the patient is aware of the cause and mental illness they suffer from, and that it's a battle for them if they want to overcome it.

Take note that OCD isn't just common. It's just a symptom of a more serious problem. OCD is described as an anxiety issue and stress is the main reason for your OCD behavior. It's not likely that to conquer your OCD until you've solved the root of the problem you're having to deal with. In the present, all is necessary is to minimize the negative consequences of your OCD to the greatest extent feasible while trying to determine the root cause of the problem.

* Many OCD sufferers have a deep angry and suppressed anger. Since anger is a feeling that must be expressed for it to let loose Repressing it can result in negative effects on the patient, and eventually turn into anxiety, which can impact the patient. The best way to handle this issue is to let out your stress or anger you might feel.

Discover the reason why you're experiencing feelings of anger that has not been addressed and learn how to express anger in a non-violentand secure way. When you speak out about your anger, the degree of anxiety decreases and consequently, the symptoms of OCD.

* Learn to do deep breathing. Patients can be unable to breathe when stressed. Deep breathing can help reverse this pattern and reduce anxiety levels. The better an individual can manage anxiety by using positive strategies to cope such as deep breathing more likely the negative consequences of OCD are lessened.

Take a look at the activities you perform take note of, and then identify the patterns you exhibit that may be linked to OCD and then determine which are the most unadaptive. In order to reduce your OCD behavior, you need to determine the particular patterns of behavior which cause the most stress for you and those in your immediate family. These behaviors should be at the high list of things you must eliminate. Your primary goal should be the transformation of these behavior patterns first.

* Join forums and sites that deal with OCD. Knowing that you're not the only one and that there are people who are around you can help you feel less alone . It'll help you realize that you're not alone person who is fighting OCD.

When it feasible, attempt to fill your time with something different from your normal routine. It is possible to reward yourself by doing things like going to the movies at the mall, going for an exercise walk, reading a book, or having an invigorating bath and playing games. Games, for example will require your attention, and also divert your mind from the problems that come with OCD.

Don't allow your thoughts to dictate your decisions. If you're thinking of something that could have something to do with the illness, you must immediately recognize the thoughts as an OCD thoughts , so that you can end it. Instead of focusing with these thoughts, change towards the other direction thoughts and visualize happy memories, such as the last time you went to the ocean or spent time with your friends or enjoyed a special event. Focus on the details of these events to help you stay free from OCD thoughts.

• Work out at home, or at the gym. Music is an excellent method to unwind. You can crank up the volume so that you are able to drown out the OCD thoughts.

Make an effort to complete something you've thought about doing for a time, but you've been unable to do it. Now is the time to make a decision based on your mood. It it will also give you an opportunity to benefit from your OCD unproductive time.

It is possible to gradually let go of your OCD routines. There are numerous occasions when you can gradually get rid of OCD routines that cause various symptoms that turn into chaos. Take note that it could require some time before you can achieve complete recovery, or even reduce the OCD symptoms you're experiencing. If you're experiencing more anxiety-related symptoms, you should be able to engage in your OCD-related activities. While you're at it, you should think about the improvements you've made in the course of your progress.

2nd Treatment, Second Treatment Preventing exposure and response

What is Exposure and Response Prevention (ERP) or ERP is one of two types of cognitive behavioral therapy or CBT. The ERP method is used to stop compulsive fear from getting more severe. It is thought that being placed in stressful circumstances for prolonged periods will trigger the brain to adjust to stress, adapting to the environment and then releasing the anxiety. This method demands the patient to confront what they are afraid of the most (exposure) however, it also stops them from engaging in compulsive routines such as cleaning, checking and long rituals (response to prevention) before waiting to see if the stress will diminish.

In general, it's ideal to complete the task by taking small, simple steps such as:

Note: On a sheet paper, write down the things that you are scared of or that you want to avoid.

Sort them in order, beginning with the weakest fears at the bottom with the most powerful ones at the top.

After you've finished making your checklist, you're able to start taking them each step at a time and begin at the bottom , and then moving upwards. Don't try to move on to your next task until you've completed the previous step.

The process of writing down your concerns is something you must complete in the span of one to two weeks max. When you've compiled your list, make sure you make it available for an amount of time long enough that you can feel your anxiety drop by less than half of the quantity that was on the list. It should take between 30-60 minutes in the beginning. It's beneficial to note your anxieties every five minutes to ensure that you'll get a clear picture of how your anxiety levels fluctuate and alter.

While you may seek help from your therapist in the process, you'll be required to do most of the tasks on your own. It is essential to ensure that the pace of the procedure is one that you feel comfortable with. It is not necessary to be in an hurried manner. The most important thing to remember in mind is that you're trying not to get rid of your anxiety but you're trying to manage it more effectively. Be aware that the main reason behind anxiousness is because it could be uncomfortable, but it isn't harmful or long-lasting. They are easier to manage if they're frequently performed.

There are two options to test using this method The ERP method:

* Self-Help. Of course, it has to be supported by appropriate instructions. It is possible to find this information via a book, tape DVD, video, or software. It is also important to maintain regular contact with a therapist or a professional, to get the help you need but it is crucial to ensure you don't go overboard often. This is beneficial for people who have mild symptoms of OCD as well as for someone who has the self-confidence to look into ways to help yourself.

"Regular Professional Contact" or as part of a team or as an individual part of an organisation. You can conduct it in-person or on the phone. In the beginning, it is typically conducted twice or once each week for meetings that last between 45 minutes to 1 hour. In the beginning, you'll require at least 10 hours of communication however it is possible that you will require more.

Third Treatment The Third Treatment is Cognitive Therapy.

It is a type of therapy for mental issues that helps you change your response to your thoughts instead of completely eliminating the thoughts. It is beneficial to those who have obsessive thoughts that don't stop, yet they aren't involved in any activity or routines that make you relax. It can be added to ERP in order to defeat OCD. The primary goals are:

* Self-critical thinking Similar to the following:

The exaggerated likelihood of something tragic occurring

Too much emphasis is given to thoughts and worries that run through our thoughts

Every effort is made to minimize any possibility that could affect your family member's lives as well as loved ones

Accepting responsibility for incidents that are tragic or bad events , even if they cannot be avoided

* Insidious and unpleasant thoughts

CT helps to develop the view of life from a different perspective. Patients are reminded of the unfortunate things that happen to them in their lives but aren't the ones who cause them to be bad people. They are also reminded that bad things occur, and getting rid of these thoughts won't help the patient. Simply relax when you are surrounded by negative thoughts and accept them with joy and moderate amount of interest. If more than one of these don't fight them and treat them the way you would treat other.

CT assists patients to identify specific thoughts in their mind. Cognitive therapists can assist in helping patients decide on which ideas they should alter and help develop new ideas that are more realistic, balanced and useful.

A majority CT meetings that you take part in will be held at your nearby GP clinic or in an area clinic. Sometimes, you may even attend them at the hospital. Making use of the phone or connecting via video calls can be beneficial if the patient isn't sure if they're ready to go out.

Massed Exposure, as well as medication - two strategies that are equally effective

A Massed Exposure method as well as standard medication are two of the most effective treatments to deal OCD. OCD.

ME is similar as ERP is a procedure which involves the writing of a personalized document of the patient's thoughts and desires. The main purpose is to uncover what's going on in your mind as a patient. The process involves three steps.

* In the context of ERP, an obsession medium is the ideal and most efficient approach when the focus is placed on an image. In this case, an image is the ideal choice to make.

The third option is to make the fear seem more insidious than it really is. It is accomplished by expressing the fear in a public way , recording the fears, watching videos or creating scrapbooks on the specific fear. It could also involve visiting the site of the fear when it's a place or having it experience in person

The most important aspect of the treatment is the cessation of the need for assurance. A lot of OCD sufferers decrease their anxiety by simply stopping all requests for assurances. Therapists may offer a reassurance such as "yes your house is in order" as well as "yes the family members are safe" but they do not provide additional assurances.

The next step involves the participation of loved relatives or close friends. They are essential to ending the anxiety. A family member who is with the patient throughout treatment can significantly improve the outcome throughout the course of treatment.

Treatments for medical conditions have found to affect OCD treatment. A highly effective treatments is Anafranil, which is also called tricyclic antidepressant Clomipramine. The medication was later closely followed by more recent SSRI class anti-depressants which affect serotonin's re-uptake , which is neurotransmitter.

Chapter 17: The topic is Cognitive-Behavioral Therapy.

Cognitive-behavioral Therapy is a treatment for OCD that utilizes two proven methods of altering the person's thinking and behaviour, including Exposure and Response Prevention (ERP) as well as cognitive therapy. CBT is administered by a expert therapist with a specialization in the treatment of OCD.

A majority of CBT treatment is conducted in the workplace of a therapist with exercises. If you notice the severity of your OCD is severe it may be necessary to have additional sessions. Mental health professionals do not all trained and therefore it is essential to choose one that has been trained.

The best way to know whether you've found an ERP therapist that is right for you is to have them encourage you to take part in exercises that expose you throughout the course of your office visits. This can help you participate in exposures that don't take place at the office. Discussion about these aren't as beneficial as starting with the actual experience of exposure. Therapy's goal is to transform an experience of exposure into the state that you are able to conquer your fears and can accept uncertainty rather than fearing it.

Therapy through Exposure

The most effective psychotherapy for treating OCD is the use of exposure and response prevention (ERP), which can be described as a type of CBT. In ERP treatment patients are advised not to adhere to the compulsions that reduce their stress and anxiety. People with OCD are put into situations where they are slowly confronted with their own fears. The process is gradual in pace.

The initial step is that you list your needs and obsessions. Your therapist and you could organize them into an orderly manner in the shape of a checklist, separating them into items that don't make you feel uncomfortable. The therapist could suggest that you face your anxieties about items on your list, beginning with the most fundamental. Let's say you are suffering from an obsessive fear of germs that can be found in public areas and that your fear isn't that great in the amount you're scared of it. Your therapist will create an exercise for you, that will expose your. If the doorknob gets in your work, you may be able to. This is where response prevention factor comes into. If you don't wash your hands as quickly as you are able, the therapist will ask you to wait until you wash your hands. If you attempt to wash your hands the therapist will demand to wait for a longer the time before washing your hands. With time you'll experience delayed reactions. This gradual exposure . It can aid when washing hands, but without washing them. You will also be able to deal with your worry about germs when you go to public spaces.

It It might sound odd However, this approach to confronting your fears can cause you to create a fear or an obsession about bacteria. The brain will recognize that if you cease engaging in rituals that you avoid, that nothing dangerous occurs.

It's likely that you'll feel angry when your hands touch the knob or be a bit confused. The body is able to establish a habit and anxiety will lessen when you wait for time to pass. It's like jumping into a pool or something. When you've jumped into the pool, you could seem extremely cold. However, your body gets adjusted to cold and you'll be feeling great.

If your therapist encourages the need to be exposed for a period of time the anxiety will decrease until it isn't visible or disappears completely. Therapists can help you gain confidence and gain techniques that will allow you to overcome your fears through therapy.

Imagineal Exposure

If you're hesitant to confront situations that are real, an imaginary exposure (IE) commonly referred to as visualization, can be a successful technique to lessen anxiety to move to ERP. Through visualization, therapists create a scenario that arouses the fear people feel in daily situations. If someone is scared of going through a corridor in a way that isn't in line with an "ideal" routine, the therapy therapist might ask them to imagine themselves walking the same manner for a short period of time each day, and then note the level of anxiety they experience. When they are accustomed to the pain and experience less anxiety with time, the patient becomes becoming reduced in their sensitivity to the circumstance and can transfer the experience to real life and be a part of the next stage of ERP.

Habit Reversal Training

This method involves introducing the response awareness learning social support as well as positive reinforcement, and generally speaking the use of comfort methods. Training in awareness may include practicing the habit to tic or behavior in front of a mirror, and then focusing on body sensations and the muscles involved in the preceding and while performing the task, as well as noting and identifying the moment the moment when the behavior or tic starts to manifest. This will help to increase awareness of the triggers to improve, making the likelihood higher that the person is able to act and alter the behavior.

This is where the competitive response is triggered. The patient along with the therapy to recognize the same reaction. Someone with vocal tics who triggers the ability to trigger them can focus on tightening their muscles and mouths to prevent the tics and then repress the urge to. A person who feels the need to feel something's touch might be compelled to squeeze the arm to the opposite side and then hold it to prevent them from doing so.

This treatment method requires dedication, time and patience, not to mention in including relaxation techniques prior to beginning. The most important element to success is the assistance and support of family members.

Cognitive Therapy

Cognitive therapy can help you realize that your brain is sending wrong messages when you try to treating OCD. The therapist will guide you detect these messages and respond accordingly to lessen your obsessions and compulsions. The therapy is focused around the meanings we attach to events are not interpreted correctly. For instance, if an acquaintance walks past without greeting you, and you're not sure what the reason is, you may consider that she was rude and imagine that "Mary isn't one of the people who likes me since she didn't acknowledge me" and then you may believe that your thoughts are meaningful or even significant. The cognitive therapy approach could aid you in keeping from these thoughts and analyze the signals thoroughly and then help you to understand something more concrete or specific. For instance it might happen that "Something is going on in Mary's mind, but I'm not sure of the exact meaning behind the thought."

Cognitive Therapy for OCD focuses on the negative experiences caused by thoughts. Although most people do not think about these thoughts (e.g., "That is absurd") However, certain individuals hold certain beliefs that believe they are always relevant. Instead of being able to let go of thoughts that do not fit with their values, the beliefs of these individuals cause them to react differently and can cause them to think "I'm an unfit person to think that way!" Research indicates that believing in negative thoughts is necessary, and that the avoidance of "bad" thoughts could result in negative consequences.

Additional treatment options for OCD

Alongside cognitive-behavioral therapy, the following therapies can be used to help treat OCD:

Treatment. Antidepressants are a an element of treatment for cure of OCD. But, they are not effective in relieving symptoms.

Family Therapy. Because OCD frequently causes issues in the family or with social adjustment, therapy for families can assist in reducing conflicts within families and help increase awareness of the illness. It can also motivate family members and assist them to assist those they love.

Group Therapy. Through the interaction of group therapy, others OCD sufferers, patients receive the assistance and encouragement needed, as well as feelings of isolation.

Chapter 18: Lifestyle And Home Remedies For Ocd

Focus on the end goal and set realistic goals for yourself. Find strategies to keep your brain active. Make sure you exercise regularly. Make healthy choices regarding your food. Be sure to stick to a regular schedule of rest and sleep you require. As we become aware of the limitations we may face it is crucial to be aware and to lead an active and healthy lifestyle. This chapter will provide some suggestions on foods that can help in reducing signs and symptoms, and will help you be more in living your life to the fullest.

Tips for living a more healthy way of life

Our lifestyles are altered to stay fit when we're physically sick. Therefore, it's logical to do the same in the event of mental health problems. If we're physically ill, we're advised by our doctors to stop some addiction or other , and eat a healthier diet and rest better. This is also true for OCD. The stigma surrounding people suffering from mental illness should be a thing of the past. But, many don't know about this issue. Be aware of the information and make yourself your own personal cheerleader. Be joyful until you reach the finish line, and never ignore the possibility that a the healthy eating habits can contribute to a healthy mental health.

Make sure you maintain a healthy life. Be sure to adhere to your schedule and are on time to school as well as work, and of course the medical appointments and sessions with therapists. Surround yourself with a supportive network of help. It is essential to be supported by a group of and knowledgeable group of disorderly family members and friends. Know how to recognize signs of withdrawal physical or mental. The medication you're taking or taking can be the cause of depression and suicidal problems.

There are many community-based events that you can choose to be a part of and to attend, often at free, and other times for a price lower than the private lesson. Be in the present moment and be aware that you're capable and will be able to conquer any problems you're facing. An image, a tick or thought are trying to take over your life. Yoga, meditation and group sessions that aid you in managing your anxiety. Take advantage of these.

Home remedies to treat OCD at home

Obsessive Compulsive Disorder has been identified as a disease that has impacted the lives of a lot of. It isn't a problem for anyone , regardless of income, wealth or age. It is explained in all its aspects and can be recognized by the appearance of ritualistic, repetitive actions such as turning knobs and frequent hand washing that turns off the lights and turning them on. It is also associated with tics that cause nervousness , including arm extensions and shoulder rotations and facial expressions. Numerous behaviors and routines. In addition, there is feelings of anxiety and fear that make the sufferer perform routinely anxious behaviors that require a lot of their time and the people around them to maintain the routine at bay.

for a moment of feeling of relief, or a euphoria or feeling of tranquil.

When they are preoccupied with these thoughts, their quality of life can be affected by the disorder. Most patients or all of those with OCD acknowledge that their actions aren't rational , but they're not able to help the poor

to accomplish these. To perform these tasks. for this disorder, but OCD is generally treated medications and CBT. Because it is a condition that can manifest across an the entire spectrum of severity, treatment options may differ for each person.

We'll be seeking other avenues and approaches that one can pursue in battling, managing and resolving the problem, which is why we'll be looking at ways to assist the sufferer by offering remedies which are accessible in addition to regular medications recommended to cure OCD. Because of the numerous aspects associated with OCD the number of people people who suffer from the

The disorder also looks at natural cures and home remedies for removing the symptoms that are associated with OCD to aid them in enhancing their lives. We'll look at alternative solutions to home remedies which can aid in the treatment of OCD within this piece.

It is important to limit the consumption of Alcohol and Caffeine Consumption

Reduce your use of substances that can cause stress like alcohol and caffeine. A lot of people turn to alcohol and caffeine to alleviate the symptoms that are associated with OCD. The problem with these drugs is that they could be chemical substances that trigger OCD is that they can be addictive.

The main reason is that once the high from caffeine or alcohol is gone the person will be suffering from symptoms of hangover, or feeling jittery because of the amount of caffeine is present in their system , which can cause them to feel tired and slow and sluggish. This can lead to anxiety that can cause OCD symptoms to become intense and make it difficult for sufferers to perform and function more.

Make a plan and follow the Meal Times

The body's reaction to stress can be negative. when stressed, lacking in nutrients or hungry, it can cause anxiety and increased levels of stress. It is essential to eat your nutritious meals, and eat according to schedule every day to avoid start of anxiety and stress. A low blood sugar level could create stress in the body that can lead to OCD symptoms and. Consuming food in a chaotic way and eating fast food can cause problems , and it is not recommended. It is advised to have three meals a day in small portions Be sure to chew food slowly and take care with your food.

Marijuana

There are increasing studies published on the benefits of medical marijuana to treat various illnesses and diseases. The studies that study the advantages of cannabis are increasingly interesting for those with only a few dollars to cover the expense of purchasing medical marijuana. Marijuana

release dopamine in the brain releases dopamine in the brain, which aids people to calm down and induces feelings of satisfaction, in addition to easing tension. But, due to legality of marijuana and its availability in certain nations marijuana isn't always available to those who suffer from one disease or another. Before you decide to utilize marijuana treatment of your illness it is crucial to know the facts.

Make sure that the product you purchase is legally controlled and legal in the area you live in.

Massage

Massage for a long period of time is considered to be an effective method to purify the body and it's an excellent way to relax and relax the mind of one's. In order to reduce stress levels, it is recommended to regularly massage your body to calm your mind and ease the desire to engage in ritualistic OCD activities.

Regular Exercise

Keep your metabolism up and let the body's endorphin levels to increase regular exercise. This is the cheapest and most effective method to increase the levels of these good chemicals that are present in your body. Go out and create a plan which includes exercise 3-4 times a week. Don't skip it.

It is not just that exercise can be a great thing for our bodies and our bodies, it also aids in getting rid of the factors that can cause stress and anxiety. Improve blood flow and keep your body in peak condition by burning off stored energy. This can assist you in avoiding OCD symptoms and behaviors. A stress-reducing exercise that is effective can also be a very effective strategy.

A great method to guarantee your mental health.

Ginko Biloba

SSRIs and other OCD drugs can cause negative effects that be detrimental to people suffering from different symptoms. A negative side effects of OCD treatment is the occurrence of sexual dysfunction. Ginko biloba, a plant which can aid patients in regaining their normal lives , and also address the negative side effects of SSRIs. Talk to your doctor regarding this.

Kava Kava

Similar to marijuana Kava isn't legally legal in every country and is only permitted to certain regions. However, the benefits of Kava kava's use in managing insomnia and anxiety along with other negative effects of OCD may help those with OCD to stay away from compulsive behaviors.

At a minimum, or at a minimum, decrease the intensity or at the very minimum, lessen the severity of.

Talk to your doctor before considering making use of the kava kava supplement. is a good way to talk with your physician.

Gotu Kola

This herb has potent properties and is an effective remedy for depression and anxiety. It has been utilized for its use in Chinese Traditional Medicine and in Ayuverdic practices for a number of years. Gotu Kola is an excellent herbal supplement that helps individuals to overcome stress and OCD triggers, and allow patients to

It's easy to work with no nervousness and distractions.

St. John's Wort

A. St. John's Wort is one of the most sought-after remedies of the organic variety that has proven to be effective for people suffering from OCD. Daily doses of this herb provides a simple method to lower stress levels and allows to achieve peace of mind and more tranquil mental state.

Increased focus on the mind. This could result in a improvement in your mental health like the negative thought process, or ritualistic behavior.

There's no reason to manage OCD on your own. It is vital to have someone you can talk about the issue with as studies have proven that there's a link to OCD anxiety, depression OCD as well as an increase in likelihood of taking suicide. Find help from an therapist, a friend or a family member or even a physician if you think that you or a relative might be suffering from OCD.

Have a restful night's sleep

Lack of sleep can cause people to feel anxious and anxiety levels can rise dramatically for those struggling with OCD are not receiving the rest they require. Sleep deprivation can affect the clarity of an individual and their overall sense of wellbeing. Plan your sleep and make sure

You have to adhere to it. To ensure that your sleep space is conducive to healthy sleep habits is essential. Make sure that you do not have smartphones, computers or other electronic devices placed near your mattress. Switch off the lights and then unwind on a comfortable mattress.

Make a plan to your sleep schedule and adhere to it. It isn't easy at first to adhere to your schedule of sleeping and waking, but sticking to the schedule will result in more regular sleep and getting up at the right time. This will allow you to feel more alert and less exhausted. Sleeping patterns that are unclear and uneasy can be a sign of depression. It could make OCD symptoms more severe. OCD can be more than just a mild.

Stop Smoking

Smoking cigarettes can be harmful to those suffering from OCD The fatigue and rush and addiction that come with smoking cigarettes can be a danger for those already suffering from OCD.

suffer are affected by OCS. The tendency to make it more difficult to control the severity of patterning behaviour isn't beneficial to those who suffer from OCD.

Chapter 19: Resolving the Condition

The process of overcoming OCD is much easier when you think of OCD as a condition triggered through anxiety, which results in severe and obsessive behaviours. The first step to success is conquering anxiety-provoking anxieties and fears. Here are some helpful tips to help you do this.

It is important to recognize that the feeling of anxiety often rooted in anxiety of being lost. If you're worried you aren't sure what's in store. You should make sure that you have clear strategies for the coming days. For instance, you could create an annual budget for the upcoming year. This will lessen anxiety about finances.

Be aware of anxiety as a necessary element of everyday life. If you're not experiencing enough anxiety most people aren't competent enough to face the difficulties of everyday life. It's normal to feel overwhelmed at times. This is not something to be worried about.

Concentrate on the things you influence. If you're anxious about something, you should make a change. If you're not able to do so, you should quit worrying. Your worry is only going to cause anxiety and stress.

Remember that the thoughts you have will not require you to perform the action. If you've ever dreamed of flying to the moon, that doesn't mean you'll fly to space. It's only an idea that has crossed your mind , but not more.

The thoughts you aren't willing to get into your head aren't real. Sometimes, a terrifying thought occurs to you. Don't over-exaggerate yourself, to let the thought go. Thoughts are simply thoughts.

Get rid of thoughts that fill your mind, and you'll improve your chances of overcoming OCD.

The only thing you need to be worried about is OCD. Anxiety that is not needed can turn you a sufferer of OCD. Therefore, it is best to stop worry in a manner that is not necessary.

Stress can trigger anxiety and even fear. Therefore, don't be anxious or stressed. Reduce the fear you experience by developing courage and strength. Make sure you are brave enough to confront your fears head-on and have the confidence to confront them head-on.

Fear and anxiety are detrimental for your wellbeing. If you're scared of something or you are anxious about something, which makes your blood pressure rise, serotonin as well as catecholamine levels rise. When these chemical levels are drastically raised in your body, they may trigger a wide range of health issues, ranging from heart issues to imbalances in acid base.

Anxiety can be beneficial or harmful. It's beneficial when it's in the right amount. Anxiety that is not controlled can be harmful for your wellbeing and can result in OCD.

Reduce fear and anxiety by understanding what triggers it. Knowing what triggers anxiety or fear can aid in overcoming the issue. You can rely on the evidence and the facts that support the trigger, not only the information you get.

These are some guidelines to deal with the fears and anxieties you have. Make sure to integrate these concepts into your brain, so you can react appropriately to any trigger or stimuli you encounter, in accordance with these ideas.

Conclusion

OCD is manageable and can be effectively treated with proper methods. A method that isn't dependent on medications is the preferred approach because it reduces the chance of negative side effects caused by the medication. Based on clinical and research studies, the most effective approach can be described as Cognitive Behavioral Therapy, and specifically, the Exposure and Response Prevention (ERP) method. ERP is possible to use ERP efficiently at home with constant training.

There are numerous examples of OCD being successfully treated and controlled through ERP. It's merely being aware of the basics of ERP so that you can use it to its fullest. It's about exposing yourself to stimuli and stopping the desire to react. In extreme situations, ERP could include other techniques that fit your personal needs.

The tips and strategies which are offered can be utilized as guidelines to help you defeat and manage your OCD. It is possible to do this by embracing a positive mindset and being prepared to face your triggers for obsession every single day.

www.ingramcontent.com/pod-product-compliance
Lightning Source LLC
Chambersburg PA
CBHW071841080526
44589CB00012B/1082